If one purges the Judaism of the Prophets and Christianity as Jesus Christ taught it of all subsequent additions, especially those of the priests, one is left with a teaching which is capable of curing all the social ills of humanity. **Einstein, Albert. The World as I See It**

...what all mystical [authentic] schools have in common is that they have the same purpose. They are built on the basis that we can understand what is divine and we can approach and realize the mystical union. **Oscar Ichazo. The Challenge to Change**

Let's face it, these hidden laws [of mysticism] are hidden, but they are only hidden by [your] own ignorance. And the word mystical is just being arrived at through people's ignorance. There's nothing mystical about it, only that you're ignorant of what that entails—**George Harrison. Living in the Material World**

ROCKET SCIENTISTS' GUIDE TO AUTHENTIC SPIRITUALITY

Mike Sosteric

Version 1.28

Published by Lightning Path Press
St Albert, Alberta. Canada.
press.lightningpath.org

This book is released under the Creative Commons Attribution-noncommercial-noderivatives 4.0 International license. This means you can distribute this work for free to others so long as you properly attribute the work, and provide a link to the original materials. However, you cannot charge a fee, modify, or remix it in any way. For commercial licensing and translation, email us at contact@lightningpath.org

https://creativecommons.org/licenses/by-nc-nd/4.0/

Print ISBN978-1-897455-12-8

eBook ISBN978-1-897455-13-5

Table of Contents

Preface...7
Part One: We Need Standards............................12
   Spiritual Expectations.....................................17
   Outcome Measures...21
   It is Risky..25
   Nomenclature Confusion................................27
   Anti-standards..34
   Summary..40
Part Two: What is Authentic Spirituality?............43
   Connection Experiences.................................46
   Connection Outcomes....................................48
   Healing...53
   Awakening..60
   Activation...71
      External Resistance....................................81
      Internal Resistance....................................91
   Ascension...100
   Summary..112
Part Three: Seven Pillars of Authentic Spirituality....116
   Corrupted Connection Frameworks..............121
   Uneducated, Biased and Mentally Ill Gurus.........136
   1. Accessible and Inclusive............................149
   2. Grounded and Embodied...........................155
   3. Responsible and Non-Judgmental.....................164
   4. Empowering..170
   5. Fruitful..177
   6. Logical and Consistent..............................182
   7. Empirical and Verifiable.............................190
   Summary..195
Conclusion...197
About the Author...201
References...202

Preface

This book is a book on authentic spirituality. This book attempts to distinguish authentic spirituality from inauthentic spirituality. This book is, further, an attempt to develop standards, guidelines, strategies, and the necessary foundations upon which we may a) decide what spiritual systems and practices count as authentic and which do not, b) research and study human spirituality, and c) build (or perhaps rebuild) authentic spiritual systems.

Obviously, the book starts from the premise that there is something real and authentic in human spiritual belief and practice—otherwise, why even bother with this exercise. I describe what that "real thing" is in this book and elsewhere, but it can be stated simply enough at the outset. Real spirituality, authentic spirituality, is spirituality that **connects**.[1] Connection is a technical term, even a neurological term,[2] used to identify the nature of authentic spiritual experience. When we connect, we connect our **physical unit**,[3] and in particular

---

[1] https://spiritwiki.lightningpath.org/Connection.

[2] Mike Sosteric, "The Science of Ascension: The Healing Power of Connection" (2016).

our brain and **bodily ego**,[4] to an ocean of higher Consciousness, a "nonlocal mind" as physician Dossey suggests,[5] an "Old One" of vast intelligence, as Einstein said, or, as I prefer, a **Fabric of Consciousness**.[6] This Fabric of Consciousness exists independently of the physical unit (the physical body), and indeed independently of the physical universe. It is as simple as that. Authentic spirituality is spirituality that helps us connect to a Fabric of Consciousness that exists independently of physical existence. Connecting to this nonlocal ocean-like Fabric of Consciousness is the seed of authentic spirituality and the core of the human "mystical" experience of connection.[7] This book teaches us to distinguish between those spiritual systems and practices that help us connect to the Fabric and are therefore authentic, and those that do not.

---

[4]The bodily ego is your body's ego, which is the ego associated with your physical brain. Neurologically, it is the Default Mode Network of the human brain. See Mike Sosteric, "The Science of Ascension: A Neurologically Grounded Theory of Mystical/Spiritual Experience" (2017).

[5]Larry Dossey, "Nonlocal Mind: A (Fairly) Brief History of the Term," *Explore: The Journal of Science and Healing* 11, no. 2 (2015): 89–101, http://dx.doi.org/10.1016/j.explore.2014.12.001.

[6]For more, see BOLIGHT

[7]Mike Sosteric, "Everybody Has a Connection Experience: Prevalence, Confusions, Interference, and Redefinition," *Spirituality Studies* 4, no. 2 (2018), https://www.spirituality-studies.org/dp-volume4-issue2-fall2018/files/assets/common/downloads/files/4-2-sosteric.pdf.

This book is intended for a general audience and for a scientific and science student audience as well. This book is aimed at a) those whose spirituality is recently piqued, b) those who are dissatisfied with what traditional religions and spirituality can offer, and who are thus looking for something new, and c) those with an interest in developing logical, grounded, and scientific standards and research programs for assessing/developing spiritual systems. This book aims to expand understanding, elevate discourse, and raise the bar about what counts as adequate spiritual dialogue. Hopefully, after completing this book, the reader will feel better prepared to engage in intelligent, sensible, critical, and open spiritual discussions.

Ultimately, the goal of this book is to provide concepts and ideas that help put us, collectively, on a solid spiritual and scientific footing. The goal is to remove blind faith and spiritual authority (i.e., listening to gurus[8] and priests) from the equation, to put aside scientific prejudice, and to make authentic human spirituality the subject of open personal and rigorous scientific inquiry. Overall, I hope to accomplish this goal by showing, in an accessible way, that spirituality is a real thing, a powerful thing, and something we, as humans and as scientists, really do not know that much about, despite our sometimes pretensions. Given the rapidly deteriorating state of the world, and given some

---
[8]The word "guru" is the Sanskrit word for teacher.

of the hopeful pearls discovered in our two-decade exploration into healing and authentic human spirituality, embracing the reality of human spirituality, and wrapping our personal and scientific heads around it by engaging in open inquiry, courageous exploration, and rigorous scientific analysis, **is the only thing that is going to save this planet**. Religious traditions are not helping much (if they ever did, really), and science by itself has failed as well.[9] In fact, if anything, our current science, which is empty of human spirituality, but innovating technologically and medically at staggering and exponential rates, is pushing us faster towards the abyss.[10] If we want to halt the inevitable plunge off the precipice, the only thing left for us to do is to put science and spirituality back together again into some kind of authentic, human whole. We have to do it now and we have to do it fast. Why? Because science and spirituality united is the recipe for global salvation. Failure to immediately unite them will lead to the realization of our impending doom.

A bit overly dramatic? Maybe a couple of years ago; but now, with one million species on the verge of

---

[9]David Ray Griffin, "Introduction: The Reenchantment of Science," in *The Reenchantment of Science*, ed. David Ray Griffin (New York: State University of New York, 1988), 1–46.

[10]Mike Sosteric, "The Red Pill or the Blue Pill: Endless Consumption or Sustainable Future?," *The Conversation*, 2019, https://theconversation.com/the-red-pill-or-the-blue-pill-endless-consumption-or-sustainable-future-110473.

extinction, and human health and long-term survival at stake,[11] only an ignorant or blind (blind in the sense of ignorant beliefs or naivete) person could deny the entire world is in a dire straight. Old ways will lead to mass human suffering and eventual human extinction. Nothing we have done in the past will save us. We need a radical global shift and we need it right now. This shift starts, in our humble view, when, as mothers, fathers, children, teachers, workers, rulers, scientists, etc., we all embrace *authentic* spirituality and start practising *authentic* spiritual connection. Only by doing that will we be able to heal, awaken, activate, ascend, and transform ourselves and the planet as fast as we need to, and as safely and surely as possible.

Mike Sosteric

August 31, 2019

---

[11] GrrlScientist, "UN Report: 1 Million Animal And Plant Species At Risk Of Extinction," Forbes, accessed May 18, 2019, https://www.forbes.com/sites/grrlscientist/2019/05/09/un-report-1-million-animal-and-plant-species-at-risk-of-extinction/.

Part One: We Need Standards

Greetings and welcome to this *Rocket Scientists' Guide to Authentic Spirituality*. In this book, we are going to define authentic spirituality and examine the difference between authentic spiritualities which are spiritualities grounded in psychological and emotional truths, workable techniques of **connection**,[12] and the physical and spiritual realities of the cosmos, and those that are not.

Before we get to that, however, and if you will allow me, we would like to ask you, the reader, a simple question and that question is, "Have you ever driven over a bridge?" Have you ever pointed your car at some steel and concrete megalith and used that megalith to get you from point A to point B over some dangerous canyon, chasm, or sea? If so, or even if not, have you ever stopped to consider the engineering, labour, time, and expense that goes into the design and construction of

---

[12] Words in bold usually indicate LP terminology which you need to know if you are going to understand the text. The convention is to put the word in bold the first time you encounter it in a specific book, to draw your attention to it, but to leave it in regular font thereafter.

Usually, the first time you encounter a term, it is defined in the text or footnote, and a link to the SpiritWiki definition is provided. Sometimes, if the concept is considered "basic at this level," a simple link to the SpiritWiki definition is provided, like this.

http://spiritwiki.lightningpath.org/Connection.

something as wondrous, astounding, and complex like a bridge?

If you have considered this, or even if you have not, you will not be surprised to learn that there are literally millions of hours od **direct labour** and **indirect labour** involved in the construction of bridges. The direct labour is obvious. The engineers who design the bridge and calculate material tolerances, the suppliers who supply the materials, and the workers who sometimes risk their lives to get it built, are all examples of direct labour.

Of course, there is more to building a bridge than direct labour; there is also indirect labour. The amount of direct labour involved in bridge building is dwarfed by the amount of indirect labour involved. The engineers who built the bridge, for example, had to go to school to learn their profession. Consider the time and energy that went not only into getting an education but also into building the university and its buildings where the professors teach and the students learn. Consider the millions of hours of research effort, course construction, and teaching time that goes into the learning. Consider all the hours put in by all the people involved and you will see that the indirect contribution to the bridge that keeps you safe is far larger than the direct contribution. In fact, it is incalculable; and this is only to consider the labour and support that goes into making an engineer! When you consider the direct and indirect labour involved in supplying the materials and machinery, in distribution and delivery of said materials, and in training and supporting the workers and engineers who put it all together, sure you will agree that building a bridge is a truly marvellous and mind-boggling tapestry of modern human achievement.

Yay teamwork!

But you know, as marvellous as all that is, it does not even come close to the marvel that, despite all the millions of hours of direct and indirect labour that goes into the construction of the modern bridge, we still manage to get it right most of the time. This is an amazing achievement, especially when you consider all the opportunity for error that exists in all those millions of hours of direct and indirect labour. Total disaster lies within an easy slip of the wrist, a misplaced decimal point, a weak beam, or a faulty bolt. Despite all this opportunity for error, however, we still get it right most of the time. From conception to design, from design to manufacture, from manufacture to construction, we (and by "we" we mean the people involved in all aspects of bridge building) manage to create a bridge that not only gets the job done, but that we can all trust will remain safe and secure for a very long time. This is a miraculous achievement. To bring all that expertise together and build something as wonderful as a safe bridge is a truly spectacular accomplishment, and one that we do not stop and appreciate nearly enough. We take it for granted, but we should not. It is an amazing achievement; we should honour that achievement whenever we can.

Of course, once we do stop and appreciate the achievement, questions are immediately raised, and one of the most important questions is, how the heck is something as complicated and grand as a bridge accomplished? How do we pull all that diverse labour and expertise together to create a safe bridge? If you ask me, it all comes down to *expectation*. We, and by "we" we mean the people who use the bridges, have an expectation that the people who teach the engineers and train the workers, and the people who build the bridges and make them safe, know what they are doing and take their job seriously enough to get everything absolutely right. We expect them to do it, and they do.

It is true, is it not? We the people who drive our cars over the bridges do not take a casual attitude toward the safety of our bridges because when our lives are involved, there is no margin for error. We don't say, "Build that bridge and we'll pray that it works." We say, "Build that bridge and make it safe," period. Furthermore, if someone does not build a safe bridge, if an engineer builds a bridge and it collapses, we do not take it lying down. We research, investigate, and we figure out why. We hold ourselves accountable and we do everything in our power to make sure it does not happen again. We get better over time, and the bridges we build do as well. It is a magnificent manifestation of human potential and a testament to the power of expectation. From kindergarten to the most advanced PhD degrees, from working in the garden to building bridges that millions pass over, all of our marvellous modern success comes down to our increasingly high expectations.

This is a good thing. It makes sense to have high expectations, especially when it comes to the lives of our children and families. When it comes to our lives, we would neither expect nor allow a careless attitude of "anything-goes." We do not say, "Just build the bridge however you want, and we will pray it works out in the end." When it comes to building bridges, we demand the truth and nothing but, and nothing else will do. When it comes to bridges, we demand the engineers, administrators, and construction workers get it right *all the time*. In this, we have no tolerance for error. When it comes to building bridges (and indeed, when it comes to many other areas of our lives), we know how to lay expectations and we know how to see these expectations through to successful manifestation. There is no profound, esoteric, or Earth-shattering wisdom here. We do not fret about it; we do not moralize about it; we lay down expectations and we get the job done.

Spiritual Expectations

Unfortunately, although we have no problem assigning standards and expectations to our engineers and bridge builders, we do not seem to have the same high expectations for our priests, spiritual gurus, and religious institutions. Look around you. Certain religious institutions continue to exist despite the fact that they breed paedophilic predators![13] Look at the people who don the **Mantle of Spiritual Authority**.[14] Look at those

---

[13]Mike Sosteric, "A River of Power Runs Through Us," *Culturally Modified*, 2019, https://culturallymodified.org/.

[14]When I say that someone is donning the Mantle of Spiritual Authority, I am saying that this person is presuming to speak with knowledge and authority on spiritual topics. I am donning the mantle of spiritual authority when I write this book because I am presuming that I know enough about human spirituality that I can talk with authority about it.

Donning the mantle of spiritual authority is what your typical priest does when he puts on his colourful robes before Sunday mass. He is putting on a symbol that signals to his congregation that he is the expert and that they should listen to him. Similarly, telling people you are channelling the "Great White Brotherhood," assuming some spiritual sounding name (like Das Ram), telling the world you are the reincarnation of Edgar Cayce, telling people you are an "old soul," creating a website with a lot of religious symbols, sitting in a lotus position and prognosticating about consciousness, etc., are all things you can do to tell the world you are a spiritual authority. When you do these things, you are donning the mantle of spiritual authority.

You should understand, "donning the mantle" does not necessarily mean you deserve it. Anybody can change their name to something mystical sounding, alter the sound of their voice, modify their use of language, and claim to channel the Pleiadian collective, or whatever. They may be valid and authentic, but then again, they may not. Always remember, having a single spiritual experience or two, and

who claim to know God, Spirit, and Consciousness. What do you see? When I look, I see some authentic purveyors of truth and connection, but I also see a hodgepodge of more or less confused, more or less authentic, more or less deceptive, and more or less predatorial, priests, prophets (or is that profits?), gurus, ideologues, existential depressives, spiritual children, creeps, snake-oil salesmen, and ego junkies who have no problem saying just about anything they want, no matter how outrageous it may be, just to get your attention, adoration, and money.

If you ask me, it is bloody ridiculous.

From the bizarre and inflated ego of Osho, with his misuse of **Connection Supplements**,[15] specifically nitrous

---

immediately donning the mantle of spiritual authority, does not automatically make them real and authentic. If you are going to be a wise consumer of spiritual information, whenever you see someone "don the mantle," be on your guard. Do not allow yourself to be led astray or bamboozled. Do not be shy. Be discerning. Be critical. Ask the tough questions.

[15] A Connection Supplement is a dietary supplement (like Cannabis, Psilocybin, Peyote) or substance (like DMT, LSD, Ketamine, MDMA, etc.) that forces a stronger Connection to Consciousness. Scholars have recognized the "spiritual" importance of connection supplements (most often referred to as "entheogens") for years. J. Harold Ellens, *Seeking the Sacred with Psychoactive Substances: Chemical Paths to Spirituality and to God* (California: Praeger, 2014); R. E. Mogar, "Current Status and Future Trends in Psychedelic (LSD) Research," *Journal of Humanistic Psychology* 2 (1965): 147–66; Robert E. Mogar and Charles Savage, "Personality Change Associated with Psychedelic (LSD) Therapy: A Preliminary Report," *Psychotherapy: Theory, Research & Practice* 1, no. 4 (1964): 154–62,

oxide,[16] and his ostentatious and egoic display of 96 fancy Rolls Royce vehicles,[17] to the prognostication of priests who frighten young children with horrendous statements of hell and damnation,[18] to the bamboozlement of ancient "secrets" that are little more than elite forms of propaganda,[19] to remarkable academic frauds like the one allegedly perpetrated by PhD anthropologist Carlos Castenada,[20] to schizophrenic and subtly racist talk of shape-shifting lizards amongst

---

https://doi.org/10.1037/h0088594.. http://spiritwiki.lightningpath.org/Connection_Supplement.

[16] Hugh Milne, *Bhagwan: The God That Failed* (St Martin's Press, 2015), https://amzn.to/2I5MglH.

[17] Chapman Way and Maclain Way, *Wild Wild Country*, Documentary (Netflix, 2018), https://www.netflix.com/ca/title/80145240.

[18] As regards the Catholic Church, it boggles the mind that despite revelation after revelation that suggests that the cloistered, hierarchical, and secretive structures of organized Catholic religion provide the perfect breeding grounds for greed, paedophilia, and abuse, that the churches of this Earth still stand. What exactly is going through the minds of people, I wonder, when they hear the latest allegations, yet still drive to their church and hand over their dollars to an institution that rapes children and then covers it up. It is going to be a joyful day when the right to exist is taken from all those institutions that support, in one way or another, the oppression, exploitation, rape, and abuse of life.

[19] Mike Sosteric, "From Zoroaster to Star Wars, Jesus to Marx: The Science and Technology of Mass Human Behaviour," 2018, https://www.academia.edu/34504691; Mike Sosteric, "A Sociology of Tarot," *Canadian Journal of Sociology* 39, no. 3 (2014), https://www.academia.edu/25055505/.

[20] Robert Marshall, "The Dark Legacy of Carlos Castaneda," Salon, April 12, 2007, https://www.salon.com/2007/04/12/castaneda/.

us,[21] they talk and we listen, without much expectation or discernment at all. We let these people, these "spiritual authorities," say (and often do) just about anything they want. Qualifications are apparently quite low; a single mystical experience or two seems to be all that is required,[22] and suddenly you are on Oprah, asked to speak at a TED Talk, or discussing the "power of now." Curiously, we do not seem to think it matters who teaches us these things, and even if we do try to hold our spiritual authorities to higher standards and expectations, we do not seem to have any globally acceptable criteria by which we can assess the truth, value, safety, or even professionalism of their spiritual statements.

The irony is deep. We say, "Build us a bridge," and we demand the best. But we let just about anybody, regardless of education, training, background, and mental health tell us nonsense when it comes to religion and spirituality! When it comes to religion and spirituality, we lack even basic standards and expectations, and that is a bad thing because building a bridge to pure Consciousness,[23] G-d, Allah, Brahman,

---

[21]Alex Abad-Santos, "Lizard People: The Greatest Political Conspiracy Ever Created," Vox, November 5, 2014, https://www.vox.com/2014/11/5/7158371/lizard-people-conspiracy-theory-explainer.

[22]And sometimes, not even that!

[23]Robert K. S. Forman, *Mysticism, Mind, Consciousness* (Albany: State University of New York, 1999), https://amzn.to/2I3Kyl6.

nonlocal Mind,[24] the Fabric of Consciousness,[25] or whatever you want to call it is, if you ask me, much more important than building a bridge across water. Therefore, when it comes to building spiritual bridges, connection bridges if you like, our expectations should be just as high, preferably even higher.

When it comes to not having high expectations for our spiritual bridges, and for sometimes being gullible and easily led astray, we would not want to cast diffuse blame. When it comes to building spiritual bridges, the primary problem is not that we cannot have, nor is it that we do not want, high expectations. Who does not want to answer all the big questions? Who does not want to connect with the "higher" realities of this cosmos? Who does not want to self-actualize their full human and spiritual potential and connect with their authentic Self? Who does not want a safe and effective spiritual bridge? The answer is, nobody. The problem is not that we do not want or cannot have high expectations. The problem is we do not know what appropriate expectations might look like.

Outcome Measures

Our lack of expectations is a problem, but we can easily change that because coming up with appropriate spiritual expectations is not that hard, once you put your

---

[24] Dossey, "Nonlocal Mind: A (Fairly) Brief History of the Term."
[25] BOL

mind to it. It is something we do all the time. When it comes to a physical bridge over an expanse of water, we know exactly what to expect. We know what the bridge is supposed to do (i.e., get us safely across some chasm) and we can easily tag a successful outcome. (i.e., to cross the bridge safely). When it comes to building a bridge over water, we might say that we have clearly specified **outcome measures**[26] that tell us exactly what to expect. We can define outcome measures simply as tests of success that we all agree on.

Outcome measures are easy to wrap your head around. We can all agree that if a bridge gets us safely from point A to point B, the outcome is successful. Thus, we can all agree that an important outcome measure for built bridges is safe passage. We can also agree that in addition to a bridge not collapsing, a bridge should be aesthetically pleasing. It should look pretty and add to its surrounding environment. A bridge should not exist as a blight on the landscape. A pleasing aesthetic is thus an outcome measure for building bridges.

You can apply outcome measures to any human endeavour from sex to baking. If the sex was good and both partners had a powerful orgasm, then you have a successful outcome. If the chocolate cake you baked is yummy and everybody gobbles it up, then you have a successful outcome. There is no rocket science to coming up with outcome measures. Whatever you feel,

---

[26]https://spiritwiki.lightningpath.org/index.php/Outcome_Measure

whatever we feel, is important becomes an outcome measure. Do you care if your cake looks good? Then that is an outcome measure. Do you think it is important for bridges not to fall down in an earthquake? Then that is an outcome measure. Outcome measures are whatever you (whatever we) decide to define as a criteria of success.

Understand, outcome measures are important. Without outcome measures, we cannot have expectations and without expectations, we cannot have safe bridges, or anything nice really. Having outcome measures for a specific human endeavour allows us to have high expectations. Having high expectations, in turn, drives us to create professional and sophisticated products, like safe bridges, or authentic spiritualities.

I suppose this all seems sensible enough. We all know what outcome measures are (even if we have never named them as such), and we all embrace these measures as signs of quality work. Nobody would argue that we should not look to strong bridge foundations or yummy cake as appropriate outcome measures. It should be the same for religion and human spirituality. As a species, when it comes to human spirituality and connection, we should be able to say we have high spiritual standards, high expectations, and meaningful outcome measures.

Unfortunately, we cannot say that. When it comes to religion and spiritual teachings, we do not embrace outcome measures and high standards with the same openness and clarity as we do the outcome measures of bridge building. Who amongst you can specify with certainty and confidence what a successful spiritual experience is? Who can show measures of good religion versus bad religion? The truth is, when it comes to our religions and spiritualities, we do not have outcome measures at all. It is really an anything-goes affair.

When it comes to spirituality, no matter who we are, we have a rather uninformed, uncritical attitude. We either accept everything on faith, or reject everything on science. Either we believe, in which case we tend not to think too critically about our spiritual choices, or we do not believe, in which case we reject without much thought. Scholars also, for the most part, refuse to develop outcomes measures and assess issues pertaining to spirituality. Even those who do take a serious and rigorous interest in human spirituality tend to remain spiritually agnostic. On this planet, no scholar or scientist says, "This is a good religion" or "This is a bad religion." On this planet, no scholar says, "This religion meets expectations" or "This religion does not." On this planet, no scholar sets out expectations or outcome measures when it comes to religion and spirituality,[27]

---

[27] Well, that is not quite true. Some people do say and some people do expect. Some people do say, "Believe this, don't believe that", but their statements usually come with threats like "you'll burn in hell if you don't" or "God won't love you." Threats that scare people are, however, not the same as having outcome measures. These people

though it seems like scholars, at least, should try. But they don't. In fact, for reasons we will look at next, many people, even spiritual ones, will actively resist the setting of expectations and the invocation of outcome measures when it comes to spirituality. Why do people resist setting outcome measures when it is otherwise such a common practice? There are a few reasons for that.

It is Risky

The first reason that we tend to avoid outcome measures when it comes to human spirituality is the fact that it is risky to try and discuss and develop them, and we are often afraid to do so. Talking about religion and spirituality can be a challenge, even dangerous, depending on where you live in the world. People can have strong opinions about things and they can respond aggressively, even violently, to open or critical discussion and challenge. I've personally been called a "space cadet" and not a "serious" scholar just for broaching

---

are not thinking and analyzing. They are not being critical and aware. They are not saying, "Believe this but don't believe that because of these good reasons." They are saying "Believe this or else!" People who do this have expectations, but they do not attach those expectations to analysis or outcome measures, they attach them to threats and control. People who say "believe this or else" are trying to control how you think by scaring you into absorbing the ideas/archetypes they offer. Sadly, and despite much protestation over the years, this sort of thing still goes on. My advice to you is, do not waste your time. You can safely tune out and ignore anybody who uses threats or fear in an argument for or against a spirituality or religion.

discussion of human spirituality, and I'm not the only scholar to face this. Abraham Maslow and William James, both psychologists interested in mystical experience, have reported "collegial" resistance and censure. And verbal abuse is not the only assault we can experience. Over the course of our human history, some people have taken it upon themselves to claim that they are the only ones who have the truth. They say, "Only this God is the right God," "Only this way is the right way," or "Only this path is the right path." Over the centuries, these people have sometimes backed up their claims to exclusive truth with various forms of religious violence. As a result, many people have suffered and died horrific deaths over the centuries at the hands of people imposing their particular standards and beliefs on others.

Whether it is drama at home or at church, professional ridicule or censure, or actual physical violence and death, these negative experiences of shaming and violence make people skittish about religious claims to truth, and fearful about discussing things too deeply, or asserting claims and expectations. Out of fear for our lives, our jobs, or just because we want to avoid drama, violence, and the open disrespect from others, we stay away from spiritual and religious discussions. We avoid talking about it and since we are not talking about it, we avoid developing outcome measures.

Who can blame people for not wanting to talk about it too much? Who can blame people for not wanting to even broach the topic of spiritual standards and outcome measures? In the context of a world hostile to open discussions of human spirituality, it just makes sense to avoid standards, shy away from big claims, stay away from expectations of truth, and throw up our hands and say, "Believe whatever you want." It is simply safer this way.

Nomenclature Confusion

Fear of reactionary, superstitious, and closed-minded backlash is not the only reason we fail to develop spiritual expectations and standards. The second reason why we seem to lack common and accepted standards for authentic spirituality is that coming up with the standards is hard to do because of the **nomenclature confusion**[28] that exists.

Coming up with common standards and outcome measures is easy with bridge building. If the bridge does not fall down, you are set. However, with spirituality, it is not so easy. Ask anybody the question "what works" or "what is a positive outcome for spirituality" and you will get any number of different answers depending on the person's background and spiritual experience. Some might say that authentic spirituality "saves the soul." Others might say that authentic spirituality gets you into

---

[28]https://spiritwiki.lightningpath.org/Nomenclature_Confusion

heaven. Still, others might suggest it is all about a life of service, or that authentic spirituality makes you wise, or gives you Cosmic Consciousness. Some even claim non-attachment, attainment of nirvana, satori, or "living in the now" as a successful spiritual outcome. I keep a running tab of all the different types of connection outcomes mentioned by mystics and scholars on a page entitled "**Connection Outcomes**"[29] and that list, which as of this writing contains dozens of different outcomes, is a literal Tower of Babel with absolutely no consistency at all.

So, which is it? Which outcome measures should we pick to set our expectations? Which outcome measures define authentic spirituality? All of them? One of them? Some of them? You can see the problem. Unlike bridge building where everybody can agree on the outcome measures (if it does not collapse, it is a good bridge), with spirituality it is hard to come up with common standards because it is a confused and confusing hodgepodge. With no commonly accepted outcome measures, with the absence of analytic precision, and with a reluctance to openly discuss, we find it hard to suggest what is real and what is not, or evaluate what works and what does not. Yet, if we are going to evaluate spirituality and decide what is authentic or not, if we are going to build a safe connection bridge, we need to figure this out.

---

[29] http://spiritwiki.lightningpath.org/Connection_Outcome

I should note, I am not the first one to note this nomenclature confusion. It has been an ongoing problem for a very long time. Evelyn Underhill, a well-known and respected commentator on connection experience (which she, of course, called "mystical experience"), writes about the confusion we face when we inquire about connection experience, and the fact that despite many "lectures, sermons, tea-parties, and talks," we still don't know what it is:

> ...the genuine inquirer will find before long a number of self-appointed apostles who are eager to answer his question in many strange and inconsistent ways, calculated to increase rather than resolve the obscurity of his mind. He will learn that mysticism is a philosophy, an illusion, a kind of religion, a disease; that it means having visions, performing conjuring tricks, leading an idle, dreamy, and selfish life, neglecting one's business, wallowing in vague spiritual emotions, and being "in tune with the infinite." He will discover that it emancipates him from all dogmas--sometimes from all morality--and at the same time that it is very superstitious. One expert tells him that it is simply "Catholic piety," another that Walt Whitman was a typical mystic; a third assures him that all

> mysticism comes from the East, and supports his statement by an appeal to the mango trick. At the end of a prolonged course of lectures, sermons, tea-parties, and talks with earnest persons, the inquirer is still heard saying--too often in tones of exasperation--"What is mysticism?" [30]

Underhill was writing a hundred years ago, but the confusion she points to still persists. This nomenclature confusion makes it hard to think clearly, hard to talk in a sensible way about the phenomenon, hard to develop reasonable outcome measures, and hard to move forward.

Perhaps it sounds unreasonable or even pretentious to suggest that we are surrounded by spiritual confusion, but consider this example. Many people might agree with the statement that *authentic religions lead to enlightenment.* This seems reasonable, even clear. Authentic spirituality leads to enlightenment. Everybody can agree with that. However, even when there is apparent agreement, confusion reigns. When we ask the question, "What is enlightenment?" nobody seems to know. Recently, I read a book edited by a well-known researcher in the field entitled "What is

---

[30] Evelyn Underhill, *Mysticism: A Study in the Nature and Development of Spiritual Consciousness*, Kindle (New York: Dover Publications, 2002), https://amzn.to/2C91xNY.

enlightenment?"[31] When I search the book for the phrase "What is enlightenment," the answers I find are a mishmash of sometimes contradictory, sometimes senseless, sometimes ridiculous quotes. When I survey quotes from the book,[32] I find that "enlightenment is for everyone," and that "enlightenment is the core truth of them all." One author says that enlightenment is "the essence of life---the goal of all growth, development, evolution. It is the discovery of what we ultimately are..." and the "core truth of *all* sacred traditions." Another says enlightenment is "the realization of the truth of Being." It is "understanding the perfect poise of begin-amid-becoming" and "comprehending the unity of all dualities." Still another author says enlightenment is "any experience of expanding our consciousness beyond its present limits." It is, says one, "realization we have no limits at all." Another says it is "never casting anyone out of your heart."

Ironically, despite all the words devoted to defining enlightenment in this book on enlightenment, another pundit says we should deny the possibility of definition, saying that "Enlightenment is ineffable—beyond words, images and concepts" and that enlightenment "cannot be grasped by the intellect, logic, analysis, or aspect of our egoic-rational mental being...." Another defines

---

[31] John White, ed., *What Is Enlightenment?* (St. Paul, MN: Paragon House, 1995), https://amzn.to/3obVany.
[32] White.

enlightenment as a psychological process, saying enlightenment is "simply surrendering yourself to what is already the case." But it is also the opposite of surrender, which is "liberation" from the world of delusions as it is. Just read the the following quotes gleaned from this one single book and you'll see just how confused people really are.

> "Enlightenment is none other than your everyday mind, but realized as such."

> "Enlightenment is instant perception of truth."

> "Enlightenment is...waking up from the dream of conventional life..."

> "Enlightenment is an expression of...ecstatic release from all boundaries of consciousness..."

> Enlightenment is "true innocence."

> Enlightenment is "a process of flowering..."

> Enlightenment is "... various seasonal changes."

> Enlightenment is "Riding the Ox Home."

> Enlightenment is "to be restored to the Divine humor..."

> Enlightenment is "transcendental."

Enlightenment is "an endless process."

In the same book, Swami Sivananda Radha says "We can see that to *discuss* enlightenment is difficult," and wow, is he correct about that. You can understand why skeptics sometimes get angry and hostile with people who talk about this stuff. A lot of people are talking, but none of them seem to know what it is they are talking about. And it is not just academics who struggle with this area. I used to hang out on some online spiritual forums and there used to be a thread on the forums asking the question "What is enlightenment?" I used to watch people try to answer the question and let me tell you, it was quite the show. Everything from trite and meaningless aphorisms to paragraphs and paragraphs of verbiage were offered up as answers. There were almost as many answers to the question as there were people doing the answering. People were talking, but nobody was communicating, and if they were communicating, the stuff they were communicating had nothing to do with authentic spirituality. What was most frustrating about the whole thing was that some people on the forum defended the confusion and disarray as "healthy debate." However, I did not see healthy debate and discussion. I saw argumentative confusion and disjointed disarray. To say that confusion and disarray is a sign of healthy discourse is patently absurd. As a teacher, if none of my students can agree on a simple definition, like "What is Religion," and if they all end up arguing and disagreeing about simple and basic concepts, I am not doing my job, and they are not learning anything. There needs to be consistency and general agreement of definitions. Otherwise, discussion cannot progress.

Let us be clear. Semantic and lexical confusion, and the inability to agree on basic definitions is not a sign of healthy debate or a mature field of study, it is a sign of unhealthy confusion. Obviously, in a field characterized by this nomenclature confusion, coming up with outcome measures can be a difficult challenge, because you cannot get past the din of the babbling pundit princes and princesses.

Anti-standards

So far, we have noted that fear and anxiety and a complicated and confused view of spirituality prevents people from looking at spirituality and developing authentic standards and outcome measures. A third reason that we don't see much progress here is that sometimes we adopt **anti-standards.** Anti-standards are standards that, at first glance, look like they might offer you valid outcomes measures, but that actually divert and refocus your attention in a way that prevents you from applying critical thought to human spirituality. Anti-standards look good on the surface and may be accepted by billions of people on Earth, but underneath they are diversionary and rotten to the core. When we adopt anti-standards, we are fooled into thinking we have actual standards and measures, even when we do not. This is a problem because if we are fooled into believing we have authentic standards when we do not, we are not motivated to look any further.

One type of anti-standard that religions, gurus, and priests use is what we might call **Death Tests**.[33] Death tests are outcome measures that manifest only after you are dead. For example, many religions will tell you that their religion works because it gets you into heaven or gets you a higher birth in your next life. This death test pushes the outcome measure into the next life and says "believe me because I promise if you do, when you die, you will see." This might seem like a valid outcome measure, especially if you grew up in a religion promising heaven, nirvana, release, or whatever, but it is not because in reality, there is no way to evaluate its truth. It is like saying you will know a doctor is helping you after you die of the disease s/he is trying to cure. If this sounds absurd, it is because it is. It makes absolutely no sense at all.

Death tests are a particularly pernicious problem, especially amongst traditional spiritualities. Adopting a death test prevents you from seeing and seeking a real outcome measure because it makes you think you have a valid test, even when you do not. If you focus on the next life, you will not care how bad your life is in the

---

[33] https://spiritwiki.lightningpath.org/index.php/Death_Tests

"here and now," or how horrible and ineffective the spiritual teachings you follow really are. If you are focused on the next life, your current life could be a total disaster, and your current beliefs totally absurd, and you would accept it with gratitude and a smile, all the while having faith that, after you die, things will get better.

Death tests are not the only anti-standards humans adopt. In addition to death tests that divert your attention from developing real-world outcome measures, we also have what we might call **Life Tests**.[34] Like death tests, life tests are contrived tests of authenticity that divert your attention from inauthentic spiritual practices by focusing your attention elsewhere, in this case, directly back on you. Life tests are what happens when a religion, priest, guru, or prophet says that life is a series of tests and that you have to accept the tests so you can grow, graduate, and move on. The general message should be familiar to everyone. If things happen (bad or good), if you get cancer, if you get run over by a car, if your family breaks up, if you are confused, if you are filled with existential angst, if you are depressed, if you are injured, if you die, it is not a problem, it is a test, and probably part of God's plan as well. Instead of complaining, instead of using outcome measures to assess your spirituality, your life, etc., you accept the failure and look for the unseen lessons and hidden silver lining.

---

[34] https://spiritwiki.lightningpath.org/index.php/Life_Tests.

An example will help make the notion of a life test, and the problems associated with it, clear. Imagine that a bridge collapses. Imagine that thousands die in the collapse. Now imagine that instead of blaming the contractor, the engineer, or the city (maybe for failing maintenance), we "look for the silver lining" and "find the lesson" in it all. It was not because the bridge builder was incompetent, the materials were faulty, or the design poorly conceived, it was because "God works in mysterious ways", life is a "test," we are here to learn. What doesn't kill you makes you stronger. It was God who "called" the victims home. It is God's will that is on display in the disaster. Don't question. Don't evaluate. Just accept.

Hopefully, you can see the problem. Life tests make all events in life, even the very bad ones, successful outcome measures. A life test can even, perversely, make a disastrous bridge collapse a positive affirmation of the value of the bridge, because the collapsing bridge taught ua a lesson. A life test can even make existential depression a thing of value because with a life test, it is all one big cosmic lesson. If you have experienced some form of violence, oppression, or injustice, don't worry, be happy because this is God's will; this is Allah's plan. If everything is a test or a lesson for you, then anything, even death, can count as a positive outcome measure. A religion or spirituality does not have to make you happy, clear your depression, make you peaceful, make you healthier, deal with injustice, fight against oppression, or get you connected. Using a life test, we can construe even an incompetent engineering firm or a corrupt and violent religion as a part of God's Divine life-testing plan.

Of course, as you can see with the example of a collapsing bridge, life tests are just plain crazy. Any engineering firm that explains the failure of their bridge as an "act of God" or says that the pain and suffering of the victims is a "life lesson" is avoiding responsibility by contriving positive benefit from an otherwise disastrous outcome. Everybody is going to see that as absurd. The same is true of other areas of human endeavour as well. If somebody builds a house, we do not expect that house to fall down because of poor construction, and if it does we do not write it off as part of God's plan. We hold the builder accountable and develop better building codes.

Unfortunately, even though we can see that life tests are absurd when it comes to bridges, buildings, and other areas of endeavour, we often do not see how absurd they are when it comes to assessing our spirituality. When it comes to religion and spirituality, we accept life tests as outcome measures of authentic spirituality without question. When something bad happens to us, we immediately see it as confirmation of whatever spiritual tradition we happen to be a part of. Hindus see karma, Catholics see "God's plan," and so on. In all cases, making life lessons an outcome measure is a diversion. Life tests, like death tests, are anti-standards. If you adopt them, you are diverted from developing real ones.

At this point, it shouldn't be too difficult to see the absurdity of life tests and death tests as outcome measures for our human spirituality. Indeed, at this point, life tests and death tests should look like obvious diversions. But, if that is true, if it is so obvious, a question becomes, why haven't we seen it before? The answer is simple. We do not see the absurdity of life tests and death tests because we learn these ideas as children. As children, we are emotionally and intellectually malleable, and we trust the adults in our life. As children, we absorb like sponges. As children, we'll believe anything we are told. If you tell a child the sky is blue because it contains water behind a glass dome, the child will believe it. It is only later, as adolescents and young adults, that we develop the capacity to question and disbelieve. Unfortunately, we don't always engage that critical ability, especially with the religious indoctrination that occurs when we are children. The truth is, if you start early enough, you can teach children all sorts of political, economic, and spiritual nonsense.

Note that this shouldn't be considered a slam against parents and teachers, Hollywood writers, producers, actors, or even priests or gurus. Just like you, just like me, they absorbed the stories and lies in childhood when they couldn't think for themselves. They just aped what they learned in the past, without consideration or the skills to critically analyze. The point here isn't to blame any one person; the point is to simply say, life-tests and death-tests don't provide a good way to evaluate human spirituality. No sense in shaming anybody here, since that is quite counterproductive. If we want to develop outcome measures and standards for authentic spirituality, we have to pry open the box of our indoctrination and move beyond the spiritual tropes of childhood. That is all.

Summary

To summarize, in this chapter, we have looked at spiritual standards, outcome measures, and some of the reasons why we do not have them. As we have attempted to make clear, not having standards and outcome measures is a problem. Just like we need outcome measures to ensure bridge building safety, when it comes to human spirituality, we need outcome measures to make sure that what we're dealing with works. Having absolutely no standards and no way to evaluate the truth or authenticity of the path you are on or the phenomenon you are studying is about as sensible as driving on a bridge that was cobbled together by hacks. Maybe you'll get to your destination, but more than likely, you won't. If you want to make progress forward, scientifically, spiritually, or whatever, it just makes sense to include standards and expectations when exploring, thinking, and debating human spirituality. You do not trust your safety needs to just any bridge-building chump. You want a qualified engineer who knows how to build a safe bridge. Likewise, you should not trust your mind and body to just any spiritual authority or spiritual system. You should have the same high standards for your priests, prophets, and gurus as you do for your bridge builders, doctors, and other professionals.

Having said all that, the million-dollar question now is, how do you come up with high standards and expectations? How, when it comes to human religion and human spirituality, do you discern truth from fiction, or reality from fantasy? How do you come up with outcome measures? In other words, how do you winnow the spiritual wheat from the proverbial chaff?

I have to admit, it is a challenge. However, meeting the challenge and answering that question is not as difficult as you might at first think. **The first step** towards coming up with standards and outcome measures is to acknowledge that we need to have standards and outcome measures, even in the realm of religion and spirituality. At this point we have taken that first step. **The second step** towards developing spiritual standards and outcome measures is to distinguish between authentic spirituality and inauthentic spirituality. Finally, **the third step** towards developing outcome measures and standards is to actually set some out for discussion.

In the next chapter, we take the second and third step forward by a) defining what an authentic spirituality is and b) attempting to set out some outcome measures which can be used to assess the authenticity of a particular belief system. Before stepping forward, let us be clear, what follows next are discussion and building steps only. The definition of authentic spirituality suggested in the next section, and the outcomes measure suggested to evaluate the spiritual authenticity of traditions and practices, are not final in any way. They are intended to clarify understanding and contribute to discussion only. They are only steps along the way. They are not the final destination.

Part Two:
What is Authentic Spirituality?

As noted in the last chapter, we need to develop spiritual standards and outcome measures to help us determine the difference between spirituality that is authentic and spirituality that is not. As noted, the first step towards developing standards of professional spirituality is to recognize that we need them and, if necessary, overcome our anxieties, fears, confusions, and emotional issues long enough so we can begin to develop the necessary standards. The second step is to understand that, just like there is a difference between a good bridge and a bad bridge, there is also a difference between good spirituality and bad spirituality. We call good spirituality **authentic spirituality** and bad spirituality inauthentic spirituality. The question now becomes, what is authentic spirituality?

At root, authentic spirituality is spirituality that *connects you*. What does authentic spirituality connect you to? We can start by saying that authentic spirituality connects you to "something more" than your normal, daily consciousness and experience. We can say this because, as mystics, gurus, monks, nuns, and scholars the world over note, the experience of connection is always felt and conveyed as "something more" than ordinary experience. As Naulty and Naulty note, "there [is] something wonderful and powerful about them [connection experiences] which places them beyond ordinary experience."[35] I certainly agree with this. Connection experiences are always "more than" you normal, day-to-day consciousness. If we ask a simple question like "what does it feel like," everybody who has made a connection will agree that it felt like "something more," sometimes lots more, than their normal everyday self and experience. Saying authentic spirituality helps us connect with "something more" has strong phenomenological validity, so that is what we will say. *Authentic spirituality is spirituality that connects you with something more.*

If you accept, at this early stage, that authentic spirituality connects you to "something more," the next question becomes, what is this "something more" that authentic spirituality connects you to? Personally, I would say that the "something more" that authentic spirituality connects you to is the Fabric of Consciousness that exists independently of the physical universe, but you can call it whatever you want, like Buddha Mind,[36] nonlocal Mind,[37] Mind at Large,[38] Wakan

---

[35]R. A. Naulty, "J L Mackie's Disposal of Religious Experience," *Sophia* 31, no. 1 (July 1992): 2, https://doi.org/10.1007/BF02772348.

[36]Master Sheng Yen, *Chan and Enlightenment*, Kindle (Taipei: Dharma Drum Publishing, 2014).

[37]Dossey, "Nonlocal Mind: A (Fairly) Brief History of the Term."

[38]Aldous Huxley, *The Doors of Perception* (Granada Publishing: London, 1984), https://amzn.to/2tXEQYI.

Tanka,[39] Oversoul,[40] Ineffable Light,[41] higher Self,[42] God, and so on. However you name and conceptualize it, the experience of it is the same. It is always felt and experienced as connection to something more.

If you are uncomfortable with this talk of Oversouls, Buddha Minds, and Fabrics of Consciousness, you can keep it in the material realm by conceptualizing the "something more" **biologically**, as Abraham Maslow did,[43] or **neurologically**, as is common these days.[44] In the case of neurology, we are connecting to some aspect of our brain's functionality not normally active during normal consciousness. Whether you say it is connection

---

[39]Dr. Charles A. Eastman, "Sioux Mythology," in *The International Folk-Lore Congress of the World's Columbian Exposition*, ed. Hellen Wheeler Basett and Frederick Starr, vol. I (Charles H. Sergel Company, 1898), 221–26.

[40]Israel Regardie, *The Tree of Life: An Illustrated Study in Magic*, 2001 (Woodbury, Minnesota: Llewellyn, 2001).

[41]R. M. Bucke, *Cosmic Consciousness: A Study in the Evolution of the Human Mind*, Kindle Edition (California: The Book Tree, 2006), https://amzn.to/2IjxuaC.

[42]Yen, *Chan and Enlightenment*.

[43]A. H. Maslow, "Some Basic Propositions of a Growth and Self-Actualization Psychoogy.," in *Theories of Personality*, ed. G. Lindzey and L. Hall (New York: Wiley, 1965), 307.

[44]Andrew Newberg, Eugene d'Aquile, and Vince Rause, *Why God Won't Go Away: Brain Science and the Biology of Belief* (New York: Ballantine Books, 2001); R. L. Carhart-Harris and K. J. Friston, "The Default-Mode, Ego-Functions and Free-Energy: A Neurobiological Account of Freudian Ideas," *Brain* 133, no. 4 (28 08/16/received 12/23/revised 12/23/accepted 2010): 1265–83, https://doi.org/10.1093/brain/awq010; M. A. Persinger, *Neuropsychological Bases of God Beliefs* (New York: Praeger, 1987).

to Consciousness or connection to deeper aspects of your neurological self doesn't matter. Materialist or Deist, we can all agree that the connection experience is a connection to something more. To answer the question "What is authentic spirituality?" then, we can say that authentic spirituality is spirituality that teaches us how to connect to something more.

If you accept the fact that authentic spirituality is about connection to "something more," the question now becomes, how can you tell if a spirituality is authentic or not? How can you tell if a spirituality connects you to something more?

Connection Experiences

To make a long argument short, you can tell if a spirituality is authentic if it leads to two things, **connection experiences** and **connection outcomes**. Let us look at each of these in turn, starting with connection experience.

What is a connection experience? Quite simply, a connection experience is the phenomenological experience of connection to "something more" than your normal daily consciousness. When an individual makes a connection, they always have an experience that provides evidence a connection occurs. It is like sticking your finger into a light socket. The shock that you get from connecting with the electrical grid is the connection experience that proves to you that you have made a connection. If you do not get a shock, no connection has been made. Similarly, if you have made a connection to "something more," that is, if you have made a connection to the Fabric of Consciousness, you'll probably get a shock, and you'll certainly feel like you have connected.

The term "connection experience" is a catch-all term, and there are lots of different types of connection experiences recorded in the scholarly and spiritual literature of this planet. People have **flow experiences** which are experiences where one loses oneself in an activity.[45] There are also **unity experiences** where one feels connected to all life, and even the entire universe.[46] Psychologists Abraham Maslow studied **peak experiences**,[47] which were experiences where one connects with and actualizes one's inner Self. We also find **healing experiences** where one experiences sudden, even miraculous, psychological and emotional healing.[48]

---

[45] Arnold B. Bakker, "Flow among Music Teachers and Their Students: The Crossover of Peak Experiences," *Journal of Vocational Behavior* 66, no. 1 (February 1, 2005): 26–44, https://doi.org/10.1016/j.jvb.2003.11.001.

[46] Walter Terence Stace, *The Teachings of the Mystics* (New York: Mentor, 1960).

[47] A. H. Maslow, "Lessons from the Peak-Experiences," *Journal of Humanistic Psychology* 2, no. 1 (January 1, 1962): 9–18, https://doi.org/10.1177/002216786200200102.

[48] Emmylou Rahtz et al., "Transformational Changes in Health Status: A Qualitative Exploration of Healing Moments," *EXPLORE* 13, no. 5 (September 1, 2017): 298–305,

There are even expansive experiences of **cosmic consciousness.**[49] All of these various connection experiences are characterized by the feeling that we have connected to something more, and so if an authentic spirituality or authentic spiritual practice is leading you or someone you know to have these sorts of experiences, then that is one line of evidence that the spirituality that is leading them there is, in fact, authentic.

Connection Outcomes

In addition to the empirically verifiable phenomenological experience of connection to something more, we can also tell a spirituality is authentic if connection leads to **connection outcomes.** Connection outcomes are real and verifiable changes that occur in an individual as a consequence of their connection experience(s). Many connection outcomes are, in fact, identified in the spiritual and scientific literature. These connection outcomes range in intensity and impact from mild expansion of meaning and insight[50] through enhanced intellectual power (i.e., you

---

https://doi.org/10.1016/j.explore.2017.06.005; William L. White, "Transformational Change: A Historical Review.," *Journal of Clinical Psychology* 60, no. 5 (May 2004): 461–70.

[49]Bucke, *Cosmic Consciousness: A Study in the Evolution of the Human Mind.*

[50]William James, *The Varieties of Religious Experience: A Study of Human Nature* (New York: Penguin, 1982), https://amzn.to/2SQZ7Jv.

get smarter after you have an experience),[51] all the way up to mind-blowing epiphanies,[52] revelations, and blistering religious ecstasy.[53] There are even some rather radical suggestions of the development of special powers, like telepathy, awareness of past lives, remote viewing, precognition, and so on.[54] The ability to teleport has even been suggested, as for example this extract from the *Book of the Great Decease* which suggests that the Buddha, an individual whom we may presume achieved consistent and persistent connection, was able to teleport his body at will.

> But the Blessed One went on to the river. And at that time the river Ganges was brimful and overflowing; and wishing to cross to the opposite bank, some began to seek for boats, some for rafts of wood, while some made rafts of basket-work. Then the Blessed One as

---

[51]Karl Hanes, "Unusual Phenomena Associated With a Transcendent Human Experience: A Case Study," *The Journal of Transpersonal Psychology* 44, no. 1 (2012): 26–47.

[52]Martin Bidney, "Epiphany in Autobiography: The Quantum Changes of Dostoevsky and Tolstoy.," *Journal of Clinical Psychology* 60, no. 5 (May 2004): 471–80.

[53]Julian of Norwich, *Revelations of Divine Love*, trans. Grace Warrack (Christian Classics Ethereal Library, 1901), https://amzn.to/2I1hnyZ; R.C. Zaehner, *Mysticism Sacred and Profane* (New York: Oxford University Press, 1969), https://amzn.to/2LcdkCl.

[54]Knut A. Jacobson, ed., "Yoga Powers and Religious Traditions," in *Yoga Powers: Extraordinary Capacities Attained Through Meditation and Concentration*, vol. 37, Brill's Indological Library (Boston: Brill, 2012), 1–31, https://amzn.to/2V8ARsw.

> instantaneously as a strong man would stretch forth his arm, or draw it back again when he had stretched it forth, vanished from this side of the river, and stood on the further bank with the company of the brethren.[55]

Many of the connection outcomes are well documented in the scholarly literature, but some of the identified outcomes, like walking on water, or the purported ability of the Buddha to teleport, strain credulity. Here we will concern ourselves only with scientifically documented connection outcomes.

Identifying connection experiences and connection outcomes is a good way to assess the presence of connection and the presence of authentic spiritual practices. If a spiritual practice or tradition leads to connection experiences and connection outcomes, it is reasonable to suggest it may be an authentic practice.

To say that authentic spirituality is spirituality that leads to connection experience and connection outcomes seems sensible and logical enough. However, a challenge does exist in the sheer number and variety of connection experiences and outcomes. The issue, besides the nomenclature confusion already noted, is that not all the outcomes occur with each connection experience. Some people have healing experiences, some

---

[55]T. W. Rhys Davids, *The Book of the Great Decease - The Maha-Parinibbana-Sutta*, trans. Translated from Pali by T. W. Rhys Davids, Kindle Edition (Amazon Digital Services, n.d.), https://amzn.to/2XKQpjC.

don't. Some have peak experiences, others don't. Some have Christian style conversion experiences, others, not so much. Some experience enlightenment, others emphasize unity. No individual experiences all types of connection experiences or manifests all types of connection outcomes, at least in the same event. Having a connection experience is like walking into the Louvre in Paris and trying to take it all in, in an instant. There's just way too much to see and experience to absorb it all in one go. Because of this, it can be hard to pin down sensible conceptualizations.

In the interests of parsimony, we are going to parse the various connection experiences and connection outcomes into four general categories of experience, these being *healing experiences*, *awakening experiences*, *activation experiences*, and *ascension experiences*. These individual experiences can lead to *healing outcomes*, *awakening outcomes*, *activation outcomes*, and *ascension outcomes*.

Before going into the details, allow me to say that, as a rule, all four of these experience/outcome types should be present, though not necessarily in the same event, or within the same person, if we are to consider a spiritual system or practice as being authentic. That is, an authentic spirituality should enable all types of connection experience. Note also that there should not be much delay in manifestation. That is, these outcome measures are not things that should take forever to materialize. Like successfully crossing a bridge, these outcome measures are the things that should immediately happen to anyone when following an authentic spiritual path that encourages authentic spiritual experience.

Of course, saying these things should happen doesn't mean they will happen automatically, and without some adjustment. Many spiritual teachers provide advice on creating psychological, emotional, and physical conditions conducive to strong and positive connection experience, which we summarize simply as **Right Action**, **Right Environment**, and **Right Thought**. In brief, right thought, right action, and right environment are actions, thoughts, and environments which support connection. By contrast, **Wrong Action**, **Wrong Environment**, and **Wrong Thought** are actions, thoughts and environments which facilitate disconnection. Just like an athlete makes nutritional changes to support their athletic prowess, so should a spiritual seeker make personal and life changes to support their spiritual aspiration to connection. If you don't make suggested changes, don't expect to have connection experiences. Even so, it still should not take forever to experience simple connection experiences. If you are following a spiritual path, if you are making changes, and if you are not having even a single connection experience, consider another path.

With that said, let us turn to an examination of connection outcomes, starting with the outcome of healing.

Healing

The first connection outcome that we will address here is healing. Although healing is not always noted in scholarly discussions of mystical experience, which tend to focus on the "mystical" side of the experiences to the exclusion of other aspects, healing is definitely a thing within authentic spirituality. Healing is a consequence of authentic connection and the expansion of consciousness that ensues.[56] This isn't a radical suggestion, and in fact should be quite obvious. All authentic spiritual traditions from all over the world have a healing component. Healing is a central focus in indigenous spiritualities, for example. Traditional Sioux spirituality has a strong healing component,[57] as does traditional Seneca spirituality. A Seneca profit by the name of Handsome Lake had connection experiences (visions) which cured him of his alcoholism. From these experiences, he gained knowledge which he subsequently wrote down in the *Code of Handsome Lake*.[58] *The Code*, which is sometimes incorrectly classified as

---

[56] Larry Dossey, *Recovering the Soul: A Scientific and Spiritual Search* (Toronto: Bantam Books, 1989).

[57] Julian Rice, *Before the Great Spirit: The Many Faces of Sioux Spirituality* (University of New Mexico, 1998), https://amzn.to/2C9fM5E.

mere prophecy, was very much a healing document aimed at alleviating the toxic effects of centuries of violent European colonization on his people. In *The Code*, Lake provides all sorts of psychological, emotional, and social advice aimed at repairing his damaged culture.

Of course, it is not just Indigenous or even shamanic spiritualities where we find a healing emphasis. Neopagan spiritualities, like Wicca, place a heavy emphasis on healing.[59] Similarly, Jesus Christ, so the Bible says, spent a considerable amount of his time walking around the Mediterranean countryside healing the sick and the suffering. We find the same emphasis on healing in Islam, particularly in its mystical component, Sufism.[60] It was the same with Buddha, who opened his first sermon with a statement on the core healing aspect of his worldly mission: "I teach one thing and one thing only: suffering and the end of suffering...."[61] After making

---

[58]Arthur Caswell, "The Code of Handsome Lake, The Seneca Prophet," *University of the State of New York Education Department Bulletin* 530 (1912), http://www.rickgrunder.com/parallels/mp305.pdf; Arthur C. Parker, *The Code of Handsome Lake The Seneca Prophet*, Kindle (New York: The University of the State of New York, 1913), https://amzn.to/2H4fr8a.

[59]Starhawk, *Spiral Dance, The - 20th Anniversary: A Rebirth of the Ancient Religion of the Goddess: 20th Anniversary Edition: Starhawk: 9780676974676: Gateway - Amazon.Ca* (New York: Harper One, 2011).

[60]Farhat Naz Rahman, "Spiritual Healing and Sufi Practices," *Nova Journal of Sufism and Spirituality* 2, no. 1 (2014): 1–9; Karim Mitha, "Sufism and Healing," *Journal of Spirituality in Mental Health*, 2018.

[61]Walpola Sri Rahula, "The First Sermon of the Buddha," Tricycle: The Buddhist Review, 2016, https://tricycle.org/magazine/the-first-

this clear statement about the importance of healing, Buddha then goes on to teach the *Four Noble Truths*, which state that life is suffering, that suffering is caused by desire and craving,[62] and that the only way to end suffering is to overcome your attachments. Buddha even emphasized the importance of care and healing amongst his disciples by saying that all true Buddhists should be concerned with healing and care of others."

> One day the Buddha visited a monastery. While he was there he came across a chamber where a monk lay in great pain caused by a loathsome disease. Although there were many other monks at the monastery, not one of them was concerned about their sick brother. The Buddha, beholding this woeful situation, began to look after the suffering man. He called Ananda and together they bathed the monk, changed his dirty bed and[63] eased his pain. Then the Buddha admonished the monks of the monastery for their neglect and encouraged them to nurse the sick and care for the suffering. He concluded by saying, "Whosoever serves the sick and suffering, serves me."

---

sermon-of-the-buddha/.

[62]The Sanskrit word used to identify the cause of suffering is "tRSNA" (तृष्णा) which means "strong desire or craving," and not attachment.

[63]Rahman, "Spiritual Healing and Sufi Practices."

Illness, suffering, and healing are a central component of traditional spirituality , as we can see; but, does authentic spirituality and connection experience lead to healing outcomes? The answer to that is yes. We already noted the example of Handsome Lake, and that's only one among many. Bill Wilson (founder of Alcoholics Anonymous), like Handsome Lake, was also instantly cured of his alcoholism by a connection experience.[64] It is not just anecdote, either. In the scholarly literature, authentic healing as a consequence of connection is observed by medical doctors, nurses, and other practitioners. In this literature, we find healing experiences, conceptualized as **Caring Moments**,[65] **Healing Moments,**[66] or **Transformation Experiences.**[67] All of these "moments" and "experiences" feature "healing modalities" that emphasize transpersonal connection and "transcendent aspects of being..." [68] In other words,

---

[64]Alcoholics Anonymous, *'PASS IT ON' The Story of Bill Wilson and How the A.A. Message Reached the World*, Kindle (New York: AA World Services, 1984), https://amzn.to/2XKQNP5.

[65]J. Watson, "Intentionality and Caring-Healing Consciousness: A Practice of Transpersonal Nursing," *Holistic Nursing Practice* 16, no. 4 (2002): 12–19.

[66]Rahtz et al., "Transformational Changes in Health Status: A Qualitative Exploration of Healing Moments."

[67]Hanes, "Unusual Phenomena Associated With a Transcendent Human Experience: A Case Study."

[68]Watson, "Intentionality and Caring-Healing Consciousness: A Practice of Transpersonal Nursing," 16.

connection. When one makes an authentic connection, one is often healed in a significant way.

How does the healing that comes from connection occur? Examining that goes beyond the scope of this little book; but note, it is not necessarily in a mystical or magical way. In fact, the healing outcomes of authentic spirituality may have a lot to do with the empirically verifiable power of the human mind and, as Bobbi Parish suggests, the "spiritual discoveries... and... self-esteem"[69] gained from **Connection Practice**.[70] In other words, a connection experience a) focuses the power of your mind, b) provides you with clear insight into the root causes of your illness and c) improves your self-esteem and self-efficacy to the point where you can make the life changes necessary to heal yourself.

As far as focussing the power of your mind, you do find examples of rather miraculous healing linked directly to the power of the human mind. Physician Dossey reports the remarkable case of a terminally ill patient being cured by a spiritual ritual that did nothing more than shift the patient's mental perspective on their illness. What was most notable about this case was that

---

[69] Bobbi Parish, *Create Your Personal Sacred Text: Develop and Celebrate Your Spiritual Life* (Harmony, 1999), 21, https://amzn.to/2I4zRi7.

[70] A Connection_Practice is any technique, such as meditation, writing, etc., that helps on strengthen and purify connection. Contrast this with connection techniques which are techniques, like breathing, intent, etc., that help an individual open a connection. https://spiritwiki.lightningpath.org/Connection_Practice

there was nothing physically wrong with the person to begin with. The individual was dying because of his belief he was cursed. The doctors involved fully expected the patient to die, murdered by his own mind. Dr. Dossey treated the mental illness with a spiritual ritual which shifted the individual's perspective. Once the perspective was shifted, the patient healed on his own.[71]

The idea that the human mind, properly focussed, can heal, or kill, isn't too much of a stretch. The western medical establishment has long understood the power of the human mind to impact the physical well being of the body. This is why placebos are always a part of human experimentation, especially in pharmaceutical research. When a company is testing a new drug, the researchers always split their subjects up into two groups, one which is given the new drug, and one which is given the placebo, basically a sugar pill which has no medicinal effect. They do this because they have found that a person's belief impacts the outcome of the experiment. If a person believes they are getting a pill with medicine, that belief can have a significant impact on their actual illness. Researchers call this the **placebo effect**[72] and it is direct evidence of the power of the human mind. Though perhaps it should be called the **Consciousness**

---

[71]Larry Dossey, *Space, Time, and Medicine*, vol. 11 (Boston: Shambhala Publications, 1982), https://amzn.to/2Vs6nBL.

[72]"The Placebo Effect: What Is It?," WebMD, accessed June 26, 2019, https://www.webmd.com/pain-management/what-is-the-placebo-effect.

Effect instead. Given the well-established consciousness effect, it should come as no surprise that a connection experience, which is basically a connection to Consciousness, helps refocus the human mind and aim it towards better physical and mental health.

As noted above, focussing the mind is not the only aspect of connection that is important. Connection also improves insight and self-esteem. If you have a connection experience, if after that connection experience you suddenly understand things better *and* you suddenly feel better about yourself and your position in the world, you are thus empowered to change. When you understand what is causing your illness, and when you feel confident about your self and your position in the world, you are naturally empowered to make changes needed to initiate and enhance a healing process. This is exactly the experience of Handsome Lake, the Seneca native already mentioned. His connection experiences lead to insight and empowerment which allowed him to not only heal his own addictions and illness, but also motivated him to help his people heal the trauma of their colonial experience. This is also the experience of Bill Wilson, founder of A.A., who had a single connection experience which healed him and which motivated him to found A.A. to help other alcoholics heal through connection experience.

Interestingly, Parish's comments about insight and self-esteem, and the biographies of Handsome Lake and Bill Wilson, all point to three additional outcome measures which we find closely associated with authentic spirituality, which we will conceptualize here as *awakening, activation,* and *ascension*. When we have a connection experience, not only do we heal, we also awaken, activate, and ascend. Let us look at each of these outcome measures in turn, starting with awakening.

Awakening

Connection, which is an outcome of authentic spirituality, leads to personal healing, and a concern with healing others, as we have seen. When we are able to connect, we search for healing. Connection also leads to awakening. What is awakening? *Awakening is basically expanding awareness of reality and expanding apprehension of truth*, that is all. When you connect, you awaken. When you awaken, you become more aware of reality and truth in its various forms.

A good way to think about the awakening that arises from connection is like when you wake up in the morning. When you are sleeping at night, you are not aware of many things in your room. In fact, when you are sleeping, you are oblivious to most things. You snooze, you snore, and the world goes on around you. You are, in short, unaware of reality. This changes when you wake up. When you wake up in the morning, you slowly become aware of the environment around you. Of course, at first your thinking may be fuzzy and cloudy; however, as you shake off the fuzziness of sleep your thinking improves, your vision begins to clear, and you begin to see. The first things you may see as you wake up are the blankets on your bed and the walls of the room. However, as you awaken, as Consciousness slowly filters back into your body, you will slowly become aware of more. As you awaken, you will see and remember that you are in your room, in your house, in your neighbourhood, in a country, and on a planet. The increased awareness and the increased understanding of the room, the world, and your place in it is rock solid evidence that you are, in fact, waking up. Increased awareness of reality is an essential feature of waking up in the morning. If you are not becoming more aware, you are probably still asleep in your bed.

Awakening literally means becoming more aware. Increased awareness, it should be noted, is not necessarily an easy thing to go through. If you happen to be one of the fortunate ones with a healthy body, good job, awesome home, wonderful spaces around you, and good relationships, then waking up to reality in the morning is a good thing and you will probably welcome it, because waking up means fun and happy times for you. However, if you are not so lucky, if you exist in poverty, if you live with an abusive partner, if your parents abused you when you were a child and you are dealing with emotional trauma, if your skin is too dark for the racist world we live in, if you are a female waking up to the deeply embedded patriarchy of this planet, if your job sucks, or if you do not have a job but need one, then waking up to reality probably is not going to be such a great experience. In fact, if your reality is filled with dissatisfaction, abuse, psychological trauma, poverty, and toxic negativity, waking up will at best be a chore and at worst a positively depressing nightmare. But, positive or negative, the fact that you are becoming more aware of your reality, even if that reality sucks, and even if you, later on in the day, dampen your awareness with drugs, alcohol, or antidepressants just to survive, means that you have "woke up" in the morning.

As you can see, awakening is not rocket science. Awakening is a process of expanding awareness and understanding. Awakening in the morning, awakening to your life as it is, can be experienced as positive or negative based on the circumstances you are in.

It is exactly as simple as this with awakening as a consequence of connection—spiritual awakening, we might call it. When you are spiritually sleeping, you are unaware of who you really are and you are unaware of all the physical, energetic, and spiritual things going on around you. However, when you step onto an authentic path of spirituality and start to connect, that changes. As you connect and work towards healing, more Consciousness flows into your body and you awaken, just like in the morning, only more so. As you awaken, your thinking clears, your vision improves, your understanding grows, and you gradually become aware of a deeper and more wide-ranging reality. When you begin to wake up to deeper and wider realities, you know you are waking up, in a spiritual sense.

Just like waking up in the morning, waking up spiritually can be a good experience or a bad experience. If you are waking up in a good reality, then the spiritual awakening process will be pleasant. If the reality you wake up into is positive, if your thoughts aren't corrupted by questionable spiritual concepts, if you have lots of good support for that awakening, then you will have positive peak, transcendent, satori type awakening experiences, which we collectively call **Zenith Experiences**.[73] A Zenith experience is any positively felt connection experience. You do not have to go very far into the literature to find numerous examples of these positive awakening experiences, though it can be difficult to sort it out and recognize their prevalence because awakening goes by many different names. Thus we have **illuminations**,[74] **enlightenments**,[75] **epiphanies**,[76]

---

[73] https://spiritwiki.lightningpath.org/Zenith_Experience.

[74] James, *The Varieties of Religious Experience: A Study of Human Nature*.

[75] Bucke, *Cosmic Consciousness: A Study in the Evolution of the Human Mind*.

[76] Bidney, "Epiphany in Autobiography: The Quantum Changes of Dostoevsky and Tolstoy."

revelations,[77] **Satori Experiences,**[78] **peak experiences,**[79] **noesis** experiences,[80] **Pure Conscious Events,**[81] and even intimation of awakening experiences so profound they are referred to as **Cosmic Consciousness.**[82]

Why so many different names for the same underlying experience of awakening? There are a couple of different reasons for that. For one, the culture and religious tradition of a person influences how they understand and name the experience. A Catholic will understand a connection experience as "contemplation" while a Buddhist will understand it as satori. The name we come up with also depends on the intensity and duration of the experience. A weak awakening experience may be understood as a peak experience or flow experience while a powerful connection experience may be conceived as transcendence or cosmic consciousness.

---

[77] Paul Tillich, *Biblical Religion and the Search for Ultimate Reality* (Chicago: University of Chicago Press, 1955), https://amzn.to/2VHLBK6.

[78] D.T. Suzuki, *An Introduction to Zen Buddhism* (Grove Press, 1994), https://amzn.to/2Tp6gWG.

[79] A. H. Maslow, *Religions, Values, and Peak Experiences* (Columbus: Ohio State University Press, 1964), https://amzn.to/2U2Rhgq.

[80] Hanes, "Unusual Phenomena Associated With a Transcendent Human Experience: A Case Study."

[81] Robert K. C. Forman, "Pure Consciousness Events and Mysticism," *Sophia* 25, no. April (1986): 49–58.

[82] Bucke, *Cosmic Consciousness: A Study in the Evolution of the Human Mind.*

Zenith awakening experiences (i.e. peak experiences, cosmic consciousness, etc.) are common and great; however, it needs to be noted that not all awakening experiences are positive. As Cortright[83] notes,

> Most people think of spiritual growth as safe. The spiritual path may not be easy, but it is usually not considered dangerous. However, the world's spiritual traditions all warn about different dangers along the way, the 'perils of the path.' New and expanded states of consciousness can overwhelm the ego. An infusion of powerful spiritual energies can flood the body and mind, fragmenting the structures of the self and temporarily incapacitating the person until they can be assimilated.

We call the bad experiences caused by spiritual experiences that occur in negative environments **Nadir Experiences.**[84] Nadir experiences, unlike Zenith experiences, are unpleasant moments of stress, anxiety, anger, confusion, fear, and paranoia[85] that can lead to spiritual emergency[86] and even spiritual psychosis.[87] Nadir experiences, which when very powerful can pitch

---

[83]"An Integral Approach to Spiritual Emergency.," *Guidance & Counseling* 15, no. 3 (2000): 12.

[84]http://spiritwiki.lightningpath.org/Nadir_Experience.

[85]David Lukoff, "The Diagnosis of Mystical Experiences with Psychotic Features," *Journal of Transpersonal Psychology* 17, no. 2 (December 1985): 155.

one into a proverbial "**Dark Night of the Soul**"[88] experiences, invoke paranoia, confusion, and ugly feelings of guilt, shame, anguish, and despair.

What causes a Nadir experience? Nadir experiences are caused when connection and expanding awareness occurs in negative environments, when the individual is not suitably prepared, when the bodily ego is damaged, and when the individual has experienced trauma and psychological damage as a consequence of **Toxic Socialization**. Toxic socialization is a socialization process that is characterized by violence, abuse, neglect of needs, chaos in the home, destruction of attachments, and indoctrination.[89] If you are waking up in a bad reality, if you have experienced trauma, psychological damage, and even indoctrination, then your awakening process will likely be less pleasant. You may still have peak experiences and nature moments, but these moments will be less frequent and less intense. It sucks to say, but in negative environments filled with anger,

---

[86]Stanislav Grof and Christina Grof, *Spiritual Emergency: When Personal Transformation Becomes a Crises* (New York: Putnam, 1989), https://amzn.to/2KbTh6s.

[87]Kylie P. Harris, Adam J. Rock, and Gavin I. Clark, "Spiritual Emergency, Psychosis and Personality: A Quantitative Investigation," *Journal of Transpersonal Psychology* 47, no. 2 (July 2015): 263-85.

For more on spiritual emergency, see http://spiritwiki.lightningpath.org/Spiritual_Emergency

[88]http://spiritwiki.lightningpath.org/Dark_Night_of_the_Soul.

[89]http://spiritwiki.lightningpath.org/index.php/Toxic_Socialization

hatred, violence, inequality, injustice, despair, suppression, oppression, drama, and death, spiritual awakening is more likely to lead to anxiety, confusion, fear, depression, anger, and even hatred, especially if that awakening is occurring without good guidance and support, or if is occurring under the guidance of reactionary or even mentally ill spiritual teachers.

How common are Nadir experiences compared to Zenith experiences? It is hard to answer that question because the people who do have them are unlikely to share them for fear of what others might say. For example, as a teenager and young adult I had several Nadir experiences which to this day, thirty years later, I still will not talk about. At the time they happened I was too traumatized and confused by the experience to say anything to anybody. Later on, after the trauma wore off, I still never mentioned them to anyone. I never mention them for the same reason that others I have spoken to over the years who have had Nadir experiences never mention them. Folks don't speak about these experiences because they are afraid, often with good reason, that if they do tell to family, friends, and even "professionals," they will be shut down because of the judgmental and misinformed responses of social networks and a psychiatric establishment ill equipped to understand connection experience.

And note, it is not only because people are afraid to talk about Nadir experiences that we don't know much about these. The few researchers who look at connection experience are also not asking about them. There are many psychological questionnaires that try to capture Zenith experiences. These make statements like "I have had an experience in which the deepest truths of creation were revealed to me, or, "I have had an experience that made me more aware, compassionate, and understanding towards my fellow humanity." However, none of the standard measures capture the negative, sometimes paranoid "bad trips" that come up when we have a connection experience. Typically, academics looking at these do not include them as valid connection experiences. Instead, they discount them as neurosis, psychosis, or even schizophrenia, reject them as inauthentic, and dismiss them from further consideration. This is unfortunate, since Nadir experiences, despite their negativity, are, in fact, valid connection experiences, and they should be studied as such. Questions like, "How many people have Nadir experiences," "How bad can they be?" and "Why do people have them?" are important philosophical, scientific, and spiritual questions. We should not ignore these experiences just because we arbitrarily exclude Nadir experience from consideration.

It should be noted that Nadir experiences need not be wholly negative. Nadir experiences can lead to positive change, even "profound psychological transformation."[90] My own spiritual journey started with

---

[90] Christina Grof and Stanislav Grof, *The Stormy Search for the Self: A Guide to Personal Growth Through Transformational Crises*

a powerful Nadir experience that, when processed correctly, led to a fundamental, powerful, and positive life shift. At the same time, handled and processed incorrectly, Nadir experiences can traumatize and damage an individual's self-esteem, undermine their willingness to pursue authentic spiritual practices in the future, and even lead to mental illness. The consequence of Nadir experiences are real. It goes without saying that scholars should be taking a closer look.

Nadir experiences are uncomfortable and traumatic experiences for sure, but it is important to be aware, they still indicate awakening; consequently, they indicate connection and spiritual authenticity, just like Zenith experiences do. If you wake up in a bad reality, you become aware of the bad reality. If there are ugly truths you have to face, you will come face-to-face with those ugly truths. If your (internal and external) reality is negative, then some of your spiritual awakening experiences will be negative as well. That is to be expected. You should not discount as evidence negative experiences and negative emotions caused by increasing awareness just because they are negative. Positive Zenith or negative Nadir, both may indicate spiritual awakening and authentic spirituality.

Also note, Nadir experiences, while they do represent an outcome of authentic spirituality, *are not a necessary feature of awakening* or *activation*. Nadir

(TarcherPerigee, 1992), 31, https://amzn.to/2UtkgP1.

experiences exist only because our societies and our socialization processes are toxic and filled with violence, greed, poverty, pain, and anguish. Nadir experiences happen because we wake up indoctrinated and traumatized, in negative and toxic spaces, surrounded by abusive parents and teachers, sexual predators, war, hatred, violence, and despair, and not because we are waking up *per se*. Nadir experiences arise because of unresolved childhood trauma, current violence, abuse, toxicity, ideological deception, and indoctrination. If there were no toxicity, ideology, or pain from childhood, if the social worlds we lived in were beautiful, welcoming, and healthy, all connection experiences would Zenith experiences of joy, wonder and power. Obviously, it should go without saying, creating right environments where connection leads to nothing but Zenith experiences should be a priority for all.

Interestingly, the danger of Nadir experiences may be why spiritual teachers like St. Teresa of Avila[91] place so much emphasis on creating calm, quiet, and drama free environments, what we call right environments, or why Buddhist monks go live in temples, isolated from the chaos and drama of the "normal" world, why cocooning is such a trend these days,[92] and why

---

[91]*The Way of Perfection* (New York: Dover Publications, 2012), https://amzn.to/2Id75es.

[92]Leslie Mann, "The `cocooning' Trend Draws Reinforcement - Chicago Tribune," Newspaper, Chicago Tribune, 2001, https://www.chicagotribune.com/news/ct-xpm-2001-10-21-

establishing safe environments is so important. As mystics the world over will tell you, a healthy, safe, calm, and non-toxic environment is a precursor to successful, and positive, awakening experiences.

Activation

That people can have Nadir experiences when they are pursuing an authentic spirituality makes sense. It is easier to live in a toxic environment if you are repressed and unaware. The more aware you are in general, the more aware you are of pain and suffering, the more likely your awakening experiences will be negative. It is like someone poking your body with a needle while you are sleeping, and poking your body with a needle when you are wide awake. When you are sleeping, you are not aware of the pain caused by the needle. When you are awake, you feel and (more importantly) see who and what is causing the pain. Makes sense, right?

What also makes sense is that once you become aware of the poking, you will take action to stop it right away. As soon as you become aware of the poking, you will probably get annoyed, even angry. Then, your hands will probably dart out automatically in an attempt to stop the poking. Finally, if that doesn't work, you will stand up and try and push the poker away. This natural and automatic reaction of trying to stop whomever it is that is poking you is the third outcome measure of

---

0110210261-story.html.

authentic spirituality, which we refer to as activation. Activation is basically the natural reaction that is caused by growing awareness of the reality that surrounds you. As you wake up, as you get out of bed, as you spiritually awaken, you become aware of reality and you naturally respond and take action. Obvious, right?

It is important to understand that the nature of your activation will depend entirely on the reality that surrounds you when you wake up. Your reaction to someone poking you with a needle will be different than your reaction to a house on fire, or a dog licking your face.

The activation that occurs in the morning when you wake up is also the activation that occurs with authentic spirituality and authentic spiritual practices. When you practice an authentic spirituality, it causes you to connect. This connection leads to awakening and this awakening inevitably and automatically leads to activation, through which you change the world around you.

As with spiritual awakening, you do not have to go very far into the literature on religion, spirituality, and connection experience to find examples of activation as a consequence of the awakening that arises from connection. Bartolome de las Casas, for example, was a brutal Spanish colonizer who tortured and murdered the natives of Hispaniola. Fiske[93] offers a scathing condemnation of de las Casas whom he called the worst of the worst. There was no limit to horrors he would commit. As Fiske notes of the repressive practices of the colonizers:

> Indians were slaughtered by the hundreds, burned alive, impaled on sharp stakes, torn to pieces by blood-hounds. In retaliation for the murder of a Spaniard, it was thought proper to call up fifty or sixty Indians and chop off their hands. Little children were flung into the water to drown with less concern than if they had been puppies. In the mingling of sacred ideas with the sheerest devilry, there was a grotesqueness fit for the pencil of Dore. Once, "in honour and reverence of Christ and his twelve Apostles," they hanged thirteen Indians in a row at such a height that their toes could just touch the ground and then pricked them to death with their sword-points, taking care not to kill them quickly. At another time, when some old reprobate was broiling half a dozen Hideout Indians in a kind of cradle suspended over a slow fire, their shrieks awoke the Spanish captain who, in a neighboring hut, was taking his afternoon nap and he called out testily to the man to despatch those wretches at once and stop

---

[93]*The Historical Writings of John Fiske: The Discovery of America*, vol. 3, 12 vols. (New York: Houghton Mifflin, 1902).

their noise. But this demon, determined not to be baulked of his enjoyment, only gagged the poor creatures[94].

Las Casas, like all other nobility of the time, was part of this horror; but then, something remarkable happened. One day while in Cuba, Las Casas read from Ecclesiasticus (Sira 34: 21-23) the following words:

> The Most High is not pleased with the offerings of the wicked: neither is he pacified for sin by the multitude of sacrifices. The bread of the needy is their life; he that defraudeth him thereof is a man of blood. He that taketh away his neighbors' living slayeth him; and he that defraudeth the laborer of his hire is a shedder of blood.

Upon reading these words, Las Casas has a brief, but classic, connection experience which was followed by an instantaneous transformation in his view of slavery and a subsequent shift in his political work. Fiske provides an account of what happened:

> As he read these words, a light from heaven seemed to shine upon Las Casas. The scales fell from his eyes. He saw that the system of slavery was wrong in principle. The question whether you treated your slaves harshly or kindly did not go to the root of the matter. As soon as you took from the laborer his wages, the deadly sin was

---

[94]Fiske, 3:256–66.

committed; the monstrous evil was inaugurated. There must be a stop put to this, said Las Casas. We have started wrong. Here, are vast countries which the Holy Church has given to the Spaniards in trust, that the heathen may be civilized and brought into the fold of Christ; and we have begun by making Hispaniola a hell. This thing must not be suffered to grow with the growth of Spanish conquest. There was but one remedy. The axe must be put to the root of the tree. Slavery must be abolished.[95].

Following his connection experience, after he became suddenly aware of just how unaligned-with-his-higher-self his actions really were, Las Casas activated. He gave up his slaves and preached against the practice. *He also sold his worldly goods,* became politically active, and was a key figure and major influence not only in advocating against slavery, but in advocating for the idea that the slaves were human and had souls.[96] Eventually, he went on to write a rather disturbing book on Spanish treatment of slaves where he provides a first-hand account of a horrific genocide that left Hispaniola a ruinous and desolate waste (Casas 1552).[97] This is a far

---

[95]Fiske, 3:273–74.

[96]Bartolome de las Casas, *A Brief Account of the Destruction of the Indies* (London: R. Hewson, 1552).

[97] If you are interested in Las Casas first-hand account and condemnation, you can read the book. It is available from Project Gutenberg at http://www.gutenberg.org/ebooks/20321

cry from the colonizing demon that initially stepped foot on Cuban soil, with the point here being that de las Casas was clearly awakened and activated by a brief connection experience.[98]

Medieval Spanish colonizers are not the only people to be activated by connection experiences. Connection experiences often trigger activation. For example, Bill Wilson, who we have already met, was an unrepentant atheist and materialist who vehemently rejected belief in God and anything supernatural. He was also a chronic alcoholic who, despite his best efforts, was unable to give up the drink. After listening to his doctor tell his wife that he was risking brain damage and death, he became desperate. One day, at "a point of total, utter deflation … with neither faith nor hope, he cried, 'If there be a God, let Him show Himself!'" It was at that point he had his one and only connection experience.

> Suddenly, my room blazed with an indescribably white light. I was seized with an ecstasy beyond description. Every joy I had known was pale by comparison. The light, the ecstasy — I was conscious of nothing else for a time. "Then, seen in the mind's eye, there was a mountain. I stood upon its summit, where a great wind blew. A wind, not of air, but of spirit. In great, clean

---

[98] Mike Sosteric, "Mystical Experience and Global Revolution," *Athens Journal of Social Sciences* 5, no. 3 (2018): 235–55.

strength, it blew right through me. Then came the blazing thought 'You are a free man.' I know not at all how long I remained in this state, but finally the light and the ecstasy subsided. I again saw the wall of my room. As I became more quiet, a great peace stole over me, and this was accompanied by a sensation difficult to describe. I became acutely conscious of a Presence which seemed like a veritable sea of living spirit. I lay on the shores of a new world. 'This,' I thought, 'must be the great reality. The God of the preachers.'

As already noted, this experience instantly cured Bill of his alcoholism. It healed him and awakened him and he never touched another drop. As a consequence of this single, powerful experience, he also became activated. He went on to co-found Alcoholics Anonymous which, in its early years, fostered connection experience, but which later on succumbed to a secularization push that removed this important, and previously quite effective[99] spiritual component.

Activation, as you know, was also a thing that happened to Handsome Lake. Like Bill Wilson, he was also a chronic alcoholic on the verge of death. His connection experience not only healed him, it awakened

---

[99] B Dick, *The Oxford Group and Alcoholics Anonymous*, Kindle Edition (Kihei, Maui: Paradise Research Publications, 2011), https://amzn.to/2VPeVP3.

him to the horrific impacts of colonialism on his people, and it activated him as a cultural and spiritual warrior of his people. As already noted, based on a series of connection experiences, he wrote a healing and **Connection Manual**[100] entitled *The Code of Handsome Lake*[101] intended to help his people recover.

It is not just famous people where you find evidence of activation as a consequence of connection. In the psychological literature, they talk about **Quantum Change**[102] or **Transformational Change.**[103] Quantum or transformational change is the rapid personal transformation that occurs as a consequence of a connection experience. This transformation is a consequence of the awakening and activation caused by connection experiences. When an individual has connection experience, they awaken (they realize the truth of their life) and they become empowered (they activate) to make changes as required.

Interestingly, activation is something that is outlined by Andrew Harvey[104] as a significant feature of

---

[100]A connection manual is a manual that provides instruction on how to connect. https://spiritwiki.lightningpath.org/Connection_Manual

[101]Caswell, "The Code of Handsome Lake, The Seneca Prophet."

[102]William R Miller and Janet C'de Baca, *Quantum Change: When Epiphanies and Sudden Insights Transform Ordinary Lives* (New York: The Guildford Press, 2001), https://amzn.to/2D1gYZo.

[103]White, "Transformational Change: A Historical Review."

[104]*Teachings of the Christian Mystics*, Kindle (Boston: Shambhala Publications, 1998), https://amzn.to/2VrC7CY.

authentic Christianity. Harvey is a religious scholar, mystic, and founder of what he calls the *Sacred Activism* movement. Harvey notes, correctly, that Christianity in its original and authentic form was all about activation. His comments on the nature of Christ's work are apropos our discussion.

> Christ came not to found a new religion or to inaugurate a new set of dogmas but to open up a fierce and shattering new path of love-in-action, a path that seems now, with the hindsight of history, the one that could have saved— and still could save— humanity from its course of suicidal self-destruction.[105]

He continues

> To a society arranged at every level into oppressive hierarchies—sexual, religious, racial, and political—he presented in his own life, a vision of a radical and all-embracing egalitarianism designed to end forever those dogmas and institutions that keep women enslaved, the poor starving, and the rich rotting in a prison of selfish luxury....Again and again, Christ, in his teachings and by his example, made it clear that the only authentic sign of spiritual wisdom is a progress in the kind of ego-

---
[105]Harvey.

annihilating humility that longs to express itself in the ever-greater and richer service of all beings.

Harvey's assessment of the nature of Christ's work is confirmed by a careful reading of the New Testament Gospels. The New Testament does not tell the story of a passive shepherd of people. It tells the story of an active and revolutionary Christ figure concerned to transformt he world.[106]

In his book, *Teachings of the Christian Mystics*, Harvey is speaking of original Christian teachings, and Christian mystical traditions, but the same movement to radical compassion, hunger for justice, and action in the world (i.e., activation) can be observed in other traditions as well. Harvey finds the same activation, the same emphasis on action and transformation of the world, in the Hindu mystical traditions. He writes:

> Lord Krishna's teaching in the Bhagavad Gita also suggests another holy secret that has inspiMalevichred some of the greatest mystics of the Hindu tradition. Simply stated, the human being *only achieves union with God in all of His aspects through a fusion of contemplation and action*. God is after all both Eternal Being and Eternal Becoming;

---

[106]Mike Sosteric, "Rethinking the Origins and Purpose of Religion: Jesus, Constantine, and the Containment of Global Revolution" (Unpublished), https://www.academia.edu/34970150/.

in contemplative knowledge of our eternal identity with Brahman, we rest in God's Being, like a drop of water in the all-surrounding ocean; in enacting the divine will selflessly, we participate in the transforming activity of God, in what a great mystic of another tradition, Rumi, called "God's perpetual massive resurrection."[107]

As with Christ's example, in this Hindu tradition of active political engagement we find Gandhi's highly influential passive resistance to British colonial rule,[108] inspired by the Bhagavad Gita, which glorifies action in the world,[109] the Sermon on the Mount, and by Tolstoy's interpretation of a non-violent, but politically active, Christian core.[110]

External Resistance

It should be noted that like awakening, the activation that comes from participating in an authentic spirituality that connects (really any activity that

---

[107]Harvey, Teachings of the Christian Mystics: emphasis added.

[108]Anonymous, "Gandhi and the Passive Resistance Campaign 1907-1914," Text, South African History Online, July 30, 2013, https://www.sahistory.org.za/article/gandhi-and-passive-resistance-campaign-1907-1914.

[109]Louis Fisher, *The Life of Mahatma Gandhi* (New York: Harper & Row, 1950).

[110]Leo Tolstoy, *The Kingdom of God Is Within You (Classics To Go) EBook: Leo Tolstoy: Amazon.ca: Gateway*, trans. Constance Garnett (CreateSpace, 2016), https://amzn.to/2Dg2jtj.

connects, whether labelled "spiritual" or not) is generally a positive thing. However, negative experiences of activation are possible as well. These negative experiences typically revolve around the experience of *resistance* to activation. It is like waking up in the morning to somebody poking you with a needle, but who refuses to stop even though you are awake and telling them to stop. You wake up. You activate. You push back. You try and get them to stop. If they stop, then your experience of activation is positive and empowering. If they do not stop, if they just keep poking you no matter how hard you activate against them, or if they lash out even harder against you, your experience of activation will be negative.

The idea of waking up to pokes, and then not being able to stop them because the other person just continues the assault, is a good illustration of what's involved in a negative experience of activation, but real-world examples will make this a little clearer. For example, think of a female waking up in a patriarchal household and then activating to end that patriarchy. A female who has a connection experience, however weak, and activates against an oppressive patriarchy at home, at work, or in the general society, will experience resistance and push back. A single female activating in a patriarchal environment, a single female standing up and claiming power and authority in a patriarchal social and economic world, may be beaten down verbally, emotionally, psychologically, and even physically as a direct consequence of her activation. In some societies still heavily dominated by male power and privilege, activating females can even be burned to death, as was the case with nineteen-year-old Nusrat Jahan Rafi who was lit on fire after reporting sexual harassment in her school.[111] The patriarchal men and women that surround an awakening and activating female will, within the limits of social and legal conventions, attack to preempt the activation and push back down.

It is not just women who experience resistance as a consequence of activation. You can also see resistance to activation when young people, naturally, or as a consequence of exposure to connection supplements, awaken, activate, and begin to question and rebel against parental and teacher oppression. Teenagers that are connecting, even if this connection is confused and misinformed, awaken, activate, and challenge oppressive parental, teacher, and even governmental authorities. When they do, they are often met with psychological, emotional, and even physical aggression and assault. In other words, resistance.

Interestingly, adolescent and young adult awakening and activation as a result of exposure to connection supplements was a major problem for

---

[111] Mir Sabbir, "Burned to Death for Reporting Sexual Harassment," *BBC News*, 2019, sec. Asia, https://www.bbc.com/news/world-asia-47947117.

authorities in the 1960s and 70s when young people, workers, the lower classes, etc., were exposed to Cannabis, LSD, and other connection supplements, began to awaken, activate, and shift away from the stultifying sexuality, brutal racism, and exploitative "manifest destiny" of their "square" and disconnected parents.[112] The connection supplements of the 1960s and 70s activated a generation and fuelled a counter-cultural revolution that pushed major industrial nations to the political left, and fundamentally altered the extant power structure. These sixties hippies experienced considerable resistance from parents, teachers, and a society that simply did not understand and was not properly prepared for what was occurring to the children. Resistance was personal, in the form of family repression and oppression, and political. On the personal level, parents would belittle and assault their "hippy" children in a backfiring attempt to make them conform. There was also political resistance, as was the case with the Kent State Massacre of May 4, 1970, where four university students were murdered by Ohio National Guardsman.[113] In the end, the only thing that shut the global activation down was a conservative "war on drugs" that made access to connection supplements

---

[112]Christopher Booker, *The Neophiliacs: Revolution in English Life in the Fifties and Sixties* (New York: Harper Collins, 1970).

[113]https://en.wikipedia.org/wiki/Kent_State_shootings

illegal.[114] In this context, Nancy and Ronald Reagan's "war on drugs" was really a war on connection and connection supplements designed to discourage the use of connection supplements that were, because of easy access, awakening and activating the children. [115]

The conflict and resistance individuals experience when they awaken and activate might be called **External Resistance**[116] because it arises from external sources. We can define external resistance as resistance to awakening and activation that comes from outside the awakening individual, specifically from friends, family, priests, corporations such as Facebook and Google, the paramilitary state, etc. External resistance comes from people who are threatened, either consciously or unconsciously, by the individual and collective activation and empowerment that comes from authentic spiritual practice. External resistance is designed to either a)

---

[114]Andrew Glass, "Reagan Declares 'War on Drugs,' October 14, 1982," Politico, 1992, https://www.politico.com/story/2010/10/reagan-declares-war-on-drugs-october-14-1982-043552.

[115]With the current global push to legalize cannabis, it seems like this war is finally won (or lost, depending on your perspective). However if there is one thing that we know, those who fear connection for its awakening and activation powers never give up. It will be interesting to see how the current global push to legalize cannabis and other connection supplements will shake out in the next ten years or so, and whether corporate purveyors of these substances will be able to alter the substances in cannabis in some way so as to remove the critical properties.

[116] https://spiritwiki.lightningpath.org/External_Resistance.

suppress awakening and activation outright, or b) divert your aspirations into channels acceptable to The System.

Whether it is outright suppression or counterintelligence diversion, in both cases, external resistance exists and is readily observable. For example, Andrew Harvey says of Christianity, that "Many forces...within the 'Christian' world, block" the "glorious liberty" (i.e., revolutionary activations) that occur as a consequence of authentic spiritual practice. This appears to be true. Marie-Florine Bruneu notes that women mystics during the 12th through 17th centuries always had a desire to "ally mystical union with service to others" (i.e., they wanted to be active and uplifting in the community) but that they were "repeatedly barred from imitating Christ in his apostolic life," meaning "Their... attempts... had repeatedly been circumvented by the church..."[117] The Church, in other words, actively suppressed the activation component of authentic spirituality. The Church appears to have used three strategies to suppress this activation. They 1) pruned the mystic's teachings of heterodoxy, 2) imposed clausura (Spanish for cloister), and 3) threatened mystics with violence at the hands of the inquisition.[118]

---

[117]Marie-Florine Bruneau, *Women Mystics Confront the Modern World* (Albany: State University of New York Press, 1998), 22, https://amzn.to/2L1L0m2.

[118]Mike Sosteric, "Power to the People: How the Church Taketh Away," Culturally Modified, 2019, https://culturallymodified.org/power-to-the-people-how-the-church-

For your information, heterodoxy is, according to Merriam-Webster, the holding of "unorthodox opinions or doctrines," in this case, opinions and doctrines against the established teachings of Church. Pruning the teachings of heterodoxy means trimming thoughts and ideas that deviate from and challenge church orthodoxy. Imposing cloister means forcing the mystic into a nunnery or monastery.

These three practices were, of course, effective at containing the threat posed by activating mystics. Pruning the teachings of heterodoxy watered down the mystic's instructions and ensured that authentic spiritual teachings, that is, teachings that helped one connect, would not spread. Cloister removed the mystic and her potentially threatening (to the status-quo) teachings by enclosing and containing them in a monastic environment. Finally, the threat of inquisition brings the final outliers to heal. Who wants to be burned at the stake, after all. As Bruneau notes, "the watchfulness of the clergy, the tendency to force female mystics to enter convents, and the threat of the Inquisition or of the stake remained constant throughout the history of female mysticism."[119]

Interestingly, religious environments are not the only places you find external resistance to authentic spirituality. You find it even in the secular, scientific

---

taketh-away/.

[119] Bruneau, *Women Mystics Confront the Modern World*, 19.

world. A branch of psychology known as **Humanistic Psychology** used to exist in a much stronger form than it does today. This branch of psychology was sympathetic and open to research on forms of connection experience.[120] Humanistic psychologists were even developing forms of therapy that were rooted in an understanding an openness to forms of connection, like **peak experience**[121] or **transcendence.**[122] In other words, humanistic psychology incorporated authentic spiritual practices as research topics and were in the process of developing highly effective therapeutic tools which could not only promote personal growth and self-actualization,[123] but connection experiences as well.[124] The problem for the establishment was that these authentic therapies were quite effective at healing, awakening, and activating people. As Carl Rogers, the creator of the encounter group, points out:

---

[120] R. A. Havens, "Approaching Cosmic Consciousness via Hypnosis," *Journal of Humanistic Psychology* 22, no. 1 (1982): 105–16; Carolyn Keutzer, "WHATEVER TURNS YOU ON: TRIGGERS TO TRANSCENDENT EXPERIENCES.," *Journal of Humanistic Psychology* 18, no. 3 (1978): 77; Maslow, "Lessons from the Peak-Experiences."

[121] Maslow, "Lessons from the Peak-Experiences."

[122] John A. Blazer, "An Experimental Evaluation of 'Transcendence of Environment,'" *Journal of Humanistic Psychology* 3, no. 1 (1963): 49–53.

[123] Hobart F. Thomas, "Self-Actualization through the Group Experience.," *Journal of Humanistic Psychology* 4, no. 1 (January 1964): 39.

[124] Carl Rogers, *Carl Rogers on Encounter Groups* (Boston: Houghton Mifflin, 1970).

> Encounter groups lead to more personal independence, fewer hidden feelings, more willingness to innovate, more opposition to institutional rigidities. Hence, if a person is fearful of change in any form, he is rightly fearful of encounter groups. They breed constructive change. . . . Hence, all those opposed to change will be stoutly or even violently opposed to the intensive group experience.[125]

So what happened to Humanistic psychology? As Elkins[126] notes, humanistic psychology was, in an attempt to undermine its powerful and progressive potential, murdered by a conservative status quo intent on suppressing the political challenges that healing and activation ultimately brought. Elkin's conclusions are unequivocal.

> ... humanistic psychology lost its power and influence, in large measure, because it is inherently incompatible with the basic assumptions and values of contemporary mainstream psychology and with the conservative ideologies that have

---

[125]Rogers, 13.

[126]"Why Humanistic Psychology Lost Its Power and Influence in American Psychology," *Journal of Humanistic Psychology* 49, no. 1 (2009): 267–91.

increasingly gained power in American culture since the 1960s.[127]

At this point, you can understand why connection and authentic spirituality would lead to external resistance. Awakening and activation lead to a status quo challenge. This challenge can occur in the family patriarchy, in the class relations of society, and even in the hallowed halls of academia. Women activating in a patriarchy challenge the patriarchal status quo. A worker awakening and activating in a factory challenges the capitalist status quo. A teenager awakening and activating during adolescence challenges parental and school authority. Activation brings pressure to change and those who fear change, or who are attempting to preserve the economic, political, or familial status quo, resist and suppress activation in order to prevent that change.

There is a lot more we could say, and a lot more research that has to be done, concerning the activation that attends authentic spiritual practice, and the resistance and suppression that occurs as a result. Indeed, with the idea of resistance in mind, everything from the use of "fire water" to decimate and disconnect the formerly healthy and connected Indigenous cultures of the Americas,[128] to the creation of spiritual

---

[127]Elkins, 267.

[128]Harold R. Johnson, *Firewater: How Alcohol Is Killing My People (and Yours)* (U of R Press, 2016), https://amzn.to/2D142T4.

propaganda in the form of innocent looking Tarot cards,[129] to the Catholic Church's editing of the Christian Bible to establish a sanitized and disempowering orthodoxy,[130] becomes a subject of scholarly interest. At this time, however, we leave aside an examination of external resistance to awakening and turn our attention to another way activation experiences can be negative experiences, and that is when we experience internal resistance.

Internal Resistance

What is internal resistance to activation? As the name suggests, **Internal Resistance**[131] to activation is resistance that arises internally, from inside you. Internal resistance is the self-doubt, fear, anxiety, guilt, shame, self-deprecation, and even paranoid terror that can sometimes accompany authentic awakening and activation. People who experience internal resistance struggle with activation and awakening because they doubt the veracity of the experience, doubt their own authenticity, doubt their ability to handle it, or have deep-seated fears and anxieties that activation will lead to negative consequences, like punishment, assault, and

---

[129] Sosteric, "A Sociology of Tarot."

[130] Bart D. Ehrman, *Misquoting Jesus: The Story Behind Who Changed the Bible and Why* (Harper One, 2007).

[131] https://spiritwiki.lightningpath.org/Internal_Resistance.

so on. You can often observe an individual's activation by the presence of this internal resistance and struggle.

Why does this internal resistance occur? That is a complicated story, but basically it is a consequence of toxic socialization. As already noted, toxic socialization is a socialization process characterized by violence, chaos, neglect, and indoctrination, amongst other things. Toxic socialization is not random. Toxic socialization is designed to mould you and plug you into The System.[132] Toxic socialization ingrains in you a deep seated need to follow authority and follow the rules. Toxic socialization also ingrains in many of us terrible self-doubt and deep-seated fear of speaking out and challenging authority.

How does toxic socialization mould us, plug us in, and make us afraid to speak out and challenge authority? It does that many different ways, but primarily through violence and ideology/indoctrination.

As for violence, unfortunately, toxic socialization brings with it a fair amount of violence. Within the toxic socialization that characterizes most families and societies, children learn to do what they are told and follow the rules, at home and at school, and they are "punished" (really, they are assaulted) when they do not. At home, assaults for misbehaving can range anywhere from psychological and emotional torture (shaming, name-calling, yelling, etc.) to outright physical assault

---

[132] Mike Sosteric, "What Is Socialization," *The Socjourn* (blog), 2019, https://www.sociology.org/what-is-socialization/.

(i.e., spanking and beatings). Schools also use psychological and emotional torture, like shaming and public ridicule.[133] In some locales, schools still use physical abuse (straps, caning, etc.).

What does all this violence have to do with internal resistance? It is important to understand, those who experience various forms of assault change their behaviour and can even develop PTSD symptoms,[134] like fear, anxiety, self-blame, etc. To understand how this works, imagine I met you and, after you said hello and introduced yourself, I started screaming and calling you names. Even though this is only one encounter, the trauma of this single encounter would cause psychological and emotional damage. Specifically, it would change your behaviour and make you anxious about future contact. The next time you meet me or someone who looks like me, you would experience a residual trauma. You would doubt your self, doubt whether you should speak up, and perhaps take steps to avoid coming into contact with me. If you were unable to avoid contact, you would be anxious about the whole

---

[133] Mike Sosteric, "The Emotional Abuse of Our Children: Teachers, Schools, and the Sanctioned Violence of Our Modern Institutions.," *The Socjournal* March (October 2013).

[134] Darius Cikanavicius, "Toxic, Chronic Shame: What It's Like to Live with It," Psych Central.com, 2019, https://blogs.psychcentral.com/psychology-self/2019/01/toxic-chronic-shame/; Abigail Powers et al., "Research Article: Childhood Trauma, PTSD, and Psychosis: Findings from a Highly Traumatized, Minority Sample," *Child Abuse & Neglect* 58 (August 1, 2016): 111–18.

encounter, wondering what might happen and worried about what I might say.

This negative behavioural change and the anxiety and fear that is the result of the trauma is psychological and emotional damage. This damage can occur after only a single experience. The more trauma and assault, the more profound the damage; the more profound the damage, the more radical the behavioural change and the deeper the fear and anxiety. For people who have experienced chronic abuse and trauma as children and adolescents, the damage can be quite severe. When the damage is severe, when the trauma is profound, even the thought of speaking out or standing up in opposition to authorities, whether abusive or not, can trigger all sorts of psychological and emotional responses, including avoidance, anxiety, and even panic.

Unfortunately, thinking about speaking out and standing up is exactly what happens when you awaken and begin to activate. As soon as you become more aware of the reality around you, you become aware of the need to change As soon as you become aware of the need to change, you automatically begin thinking about how you might do that. When you start thinking about the actions you might take, anxiety, fear, and panic can be triggered, and all this can shut you right down. If one day you wake up and you realize just how abusive an authority figure in your life is, say your patriarchal father, a PTSD derived fear of authority may trigger in you and you may be come anxious and panicked as a result. You may not know why you are anxious and panicked. You may not know it is because you are having thoughts about challenging and changing the status quo, but you will be anxious. This anxiety is internal resistance. If you succumb to it, you will be deactivated as a result,

When individuals are assaulted for not submitting to the rules, whether as children, adolescents, or adults, we call this **oppression**. Oppression is a form of action designed to neutralize activation and disempower individuals by traumatizing and instilling fear. Oppression and the psychological trauma that goes along with it are key sources of internal resistance. If you are afraid of standing up and speaking out because of what your parents did to you as a child, what your teachers and "friends" did to you at school, or what your bosses do to you at work, you are oppressed and less likely to experience an empowering, positive, and trouble-free activation.

As noted above, toxic socialization moulds us, plugs us into The System, and often makes us afraid to speak out and challenge authority. It does this via violence, as already discussed, and also *ideology and indoctrination.* Ideology is ideas taught to us as children and adolescents that dis-empower us and work against awakening and activation in sometimes overt, sometimes subtle, but always very powerful ways. These ideologies are most obvious in Christian instructions that teach you will be forever damned for not following the authority and commandments of God, and also in Vedic notions of Karma, which also suggest punishment (i.e. a lower birth) for not following the rules. However, ancient Christian notions of hell and damnation and Vedic notions of karma and rebirth are not the only punishment based ideas that impact activation. These ideas also exist in the New Age movement where we are told that we are stupid, fallen, weak, worthless, primitive, unworthy, and sinful rejects who are incarnated here on Earth to learn spiritual "lessons" so we can graduate and evolve to the next level. We also find these ideological messages in science where we are told that we are biologically rooted to a violent, "survival of the fittest" ape-thing past.

We call ideological messages that teach us that we are sinful, rotten, bad actors who should follow authority, and who need punishment and correction, **Less Than Messages (LTM's)**.[135] Less than messages are the constant and ubiquitous aspersions cast upon us by a spiritual, esoteric, and scientific culture designed to prevent awakening, activation, and ascension. Less than messages undermine self-esteem and self-efficacy, confuse you, and generally send you off down dead end roads that lead no where but the grave. Less than messages form the foundation of internal conflict and

---

[135] https://spiritwiki.lightningpath.org/Less_Than_Messages

struggle which can be triggered during the activation that follows upon awakening. We absorb all these less than messages growing up, and as a consequence, when we activate, sometimes even when we awaken, we feel "unworthy," "incapable," "sinful," and so on. These thoughts and emotions can undermine and even reverse what could otherwise be a productive and positive awakening and activation experience.

As with our examination of external resistance, a lot more could be said about the ideas and ideology which fuel internal resistance. We will examine the ideological underpinning of internal resistance at a later date when we explore the "old energy" archetypal fabric of this planet. As a general statement, anybody who has had a connection experience will be likely attest to both the awakening and activation components of the connection experience, as well as the Zenith and Nadir experiences, and the internal and external resistance one may experience. It is up to researchers to quit dismissing negative aspects of connection experience.

As for the personal experiences themselves, if you do have a Nadir experience, or if you experience resistance, either external or internal, pay attention and, if necessary, get appropriate help. If you are experiencing external resistance, find an appropriate support group, for example. For people in abusive relationships, this would be a relationship support group. For adolescents experiencing trauma and violence at home or at school, this may be a professional support worker, a gay-straight alliance, or some other type of professionally guided peer support group. Similarly, if you experience internal resistance, seek psychological assistance. Seeking psychological help is particularly important if the activation is triggering acute PTSD like symptoms (i.e. anxiety, distress, sleep disruption, toxic and negative ideations), neurosis, or even psychosis (confusion, paranoia, etc.).

If you do experience internal resistance, interrogate your spiritual ideology to see where negative, self-limiting, and paranoia-inducing thoughts are coming from. Interrogating your spirituality means examining your thought processes and looking for ideas that you don't want to think, like "less than messages" that undermine your self-esteem and self-efficacy, and that make awakening and activation difficult. When you find those ideas, engage in a process of **mental purification,** or just purification for short, to clear them up. Purification is simply the identification and extraction of thoughts and concepts that disempower and disconnect.

Mental purification is a complicated process, but it basically comes down to being *mindful* of your thoughts and feelings, being *attentive* to the thoughts that affect your feelings in a negative way, and being *active* in trying to replace those thoughts that diminish you. If you have an awakening experience and then a couple days later you are feeling slightly depressed, or are dealing with thoughts of self-doubt, pay attention to what you are thinking. Write your thoughts down. Once you have identified self-limiting, negative thoughts and images, you can work to clear the self-limiting ideas and archetypes with more empowering and expansive ones. It is a big process, a challenging one, and I'll go into more detail at a later date. For now, just get started with mindfulness training, and get used to noting the ideas and feelings you have. This work will help you overcome some of the internal resistance you may experience if you happen to have an authentic connection experience.

As a final note to this section on activation, the idea that you might have to interrogate your thoughts, emotions, and ideas, i.e. that you have to to work to establish right thought, may sound a little strange, but it actually has ancient precedent in the sacred and spiritual literature of this planet. Esteemed Vedic teacher Sankaracharya speaks of the purification of one's thoughts[136] as a necessary step on an authentic spiritual path. The Buddhist **Noble Eightfold Path** also contains strong guidance on the importance of "Right Thought," "Right Understanding," "Right Concentration," and "Right Mindfulness,"[137] all of which speak to the

---

[136]Sankaracharya, *The Crest-Jewel of Wisdom and Other Writings of Sankaracharya*, trans. Charles Johnston, Kindle Edition (1999: Theosophical University Press, 1946), https://www.theosociety.org/pasadena/crest/crest-1.htm.

[137]Walpola Sri Rahula, "The Noble Eightfold Path: Meaning and Practice," Tricycle: The Buddhist Review, accessed April 25, 2019,

importance of mental purification and mental discipline. Similar advice has been given to Christian mystics down through the ages as well. For example, John Climacus,[138] a 6th-century Christian monk, tell us to excise "evil," "polluted" and "profane" thoughts so that we can make pure connections with Consciousness. Similarly, St. Teresa of Avila spends considerable time teaching detachment, the avoidance of stress and negativity, and mental discipline as requisite achievements on the path to powerful contemplation (i.e. connection).[139]

Ascension

As the reader will by now be well aware, this book is a book on authentic spirituality which, as you now know, is a spirituality that teaches and supports building a bridge of connection to "something more" than our normal, daily, self and consciousness. This is also a book about how to identify connection and how to determine when a spirituality is authentic or not. As we have seen, one way to determine the authenticity of a spirituality or spiritual practice is to look for connection outcomes. Three connection outcomes identified so far are **healing, awakening**, and **activation**. As we have seen, there is lots of evidence in the literature to suggest that healing, awakening, and activation are basic features of authentic

---

https://tricycle.org/magazine/noble-eightfold-path/.

[138]*The Ladder of Divine Ascent* (Toronto: Patristic Publishing, 2017).

[139]St. Teresa of Avila, *The Way of Perfection*.

spirituality, and so when we are evaluating an authentic spirituality or spiritual practice, we need to look for examples of each.

Healing, awakening, and activation are important connection outcomes, but that is not the end of the story. A fourth and final outcome measure we are going to examine here is the outcome measure of ascension. What is ascension? Recall our earlier definition of authentic spirituality. Authentic spirituality connects you to "something more" than your normal consciousness. This connection is highly significant and can lead to insights, dramatic realizations, enlightenments, epiphanies, expansion of consciousness, and finally *union* (more or less) with this "something more." The process of expansion, healing, awakening, epiphany, enlightenment, and challenge that leads, if pursued persistently and consistently, to "union" with this "something more" is the process of ascension. Defining the term ascension we would say that *ascension is the process of pursuing union with whatever the "something more" is that one is connecting to.*

Why do we use the word ascension? For one, it fits linguistically, even poetically, with awakening and activation. For two, and more importantly, it fits phenomenologically with the experience. That is, to the people undergoing the process, it actually feels like an ascension and union. Indeed, mystics who write about the process often speak in terms of ascent towards union, like one is moving towards something bigger, higher, and more grand than normal. John Climacus, a Medieval monk, wrote a book entitled *The Ladder of Divine Ascent* and in that book he describes not only the ascent, but how to lubricate the process and make the ascent easier.[140] It is fairly straight forward. When the ascent is completed, one achieves union with something more.[141]

As already noted, there are spiritual and material ways to conceptualize connection to that something more. In material terms, you can conceptualize connection biologically or neurologically, as connection with or activation of some aspect of your neurology. Spiritually, we conceptualize the connection that occurs as connection to something we call the Fabric of Consciousness. To refine that, we would further suggest that the connection that occurs is, first and foremost, a connection between your bodily ego, which is the neurological ego of your physical body, and the spiritual ego, which is the ego that exists independently of the

---

[140] Climacus, *The Ladder of Divine Ascent*.

[141] As a side note, sometimes this process is perceived as a descent, as in the descent of the Holy Spirit, or the descent of Consciousness, into the physical body. Thus we have "Then all the people were being baptized, Jesus was baptized too. And as he was praying, heaven was opened and the Holy Spirit descended on him in bodily form like a dove" (Like 3: 21-22). Here, the "something more" we are connecting to is the Holy Spirit, and the process is described as this spirit descending into the body.

material world, as part of the Fabric of Consciousness.[142] When you make a connection, you bring your bodily ego and your spiritual ego together for a short period of time. The more you do that, the more you engage in **Connection Practice**, the more you work on bringing the two together, the more you merge your bodily ego with your spiritual ego, the more you ascend towards union.

Why does connection lead to an ascension process? Because nobody achieves perfect union the first time they have a connection experience. People have **Union Experiences** all the time, but unless a connection is forced open by a long acting connection supplement like LSD, in which case one can experience union for hours, union experiences are usually only a few seconds. Typically, a union experience is just a brief connection that feels like a deeper union. It is like turning a super bright line on in a dark room for a second or two, getting a glimpse of what's inside that room, and then covering your eyes and turning the light back off because it's just too bright to keep on. To get to the point where you can "keep the light on," so to speak, you have to work to get your eyes adjusted.

---

[142]Sosteric, "The Science of Ascension: A Neurologically Grounded Theory of Mystical/Spiritual Experience"; Mike Sosteric, *Lightning Path Workbook One: Basic Concepts*, vol. 1, Lightning Path Workbook Series (St. Albert, Alberta: Lightning Path Press, 2016), https://press.lightningpath.org/product/the-lightning-path-book-one-authentic-spirituality/.

The reason nobody achieves perfect union the first time, or even the tenth time, is because, among other things, the spiritual ego is much bigger than the bodily ego. If you think of your bodily ego as a small candle flame and your spiritual ego like the blazing light of the sun, you'll get a sense of the issue and the magnitude. Making a connection can be like standing in a dark room and suddenly turning to face a million watt light bulb. Even under ideal circumstances, it takes time to adjust to the light. This process of "adjustment" is the process of ascension. Once you have adjusted to the bright light of your spiritual ego, or the extra capacities of your neurology, then a more permanent and consistent connection/union can occur.

Note that it is not just the brightness of the light of the spiritual ego/Fabric that is the problem. The bodily ego itself might be a problem as well. This is the case if, for example, the bodily ego has been heavily damaged by toxic socialization. For reasons we cannot explore in too much detail here, when the bodily ego is damaged and indoctrinated by toxic socialization, connection and the process of union can be difficult. When the bodily ego is damaged, the process is not just about adjusting to the light, it is also about healing damage to the self-esteem and self-concept, and clearing the wrong thought and indoctrination, which diminishes self, distorts thinking, and makes connection more difficult. It should be noted that the healing component is *extremely* important. As we will see in the next section on the Seven Pillars of Authentic Spirituality, anybody can have a connection experience, even the mentally ill. As we will see, when people with mental illness experience connection, things can go horribly wrong. Therefore, healing the mind so it can handle connection is an extremely important aspect of connection and ascension.

Anyway, you see the issue. Anybody can have a connection experience, but the thing we are connecting too is so bright that it takes work to make that connection longer and more permanent. The work involved in making a connection longer and more permanent is the work of ascension. It is important work but, sadly, not too many people go on to do it, not because they can't, and not because they won't, but because pundits don't always make the requirement clear, either because they themselves don't know, or because they have based their expertise on only a connection experience or two and thus think that that's all there is to it.

Is ascension, this process of union and merging, a thing in the spiritual and scientific literature of the planet? It definitely is. In fact, ascension is often defined as the *sine qua non* of spiritual practice, and the quintessential sought after connection outcome. Zaehnar[143] provides an excellent, if quite general,

---

[143]*Hindu and Muslim Mysticism* (New York: Shocken Books, 1969), 5, https://amzn.to/2IK1A7R.

definition of "mysticism," which is really a description of the process of ascension. As he says, mysticism (read ascension) is "the realization of a union or a unity with or in [or of] something that is enormously, if not infinitely, greater than the empirical self.[144] And of course, Zaehnar is not the only one. The concept of a process of ascension appears everywhere and in every time period, over and over again. It appears in Orphic literature, which is ancient Greek mystical literature, where the "ultimate goal is reunion with the divine."[145] The Sanskrit word "yoga" actually means "union," and Yoga, in its pure non-Westernized form,[146] is all about achieving union with this higher Light/higher Self.[147] Likewise, Zen Buddhism shares the same goal. Chan speaks of the practice of Zen and how it is aimed at clearing the mind to facilitate union with Self.[148] Aldous

---

[144]Zaehnar's definition is a definition of mysticism, which is the word most people use when they think about what we are calling authentic spirituality. Zaehnar's definition is OK so long as we recognize that a) it doesn't include other important outcome measure of connection, like awakening and activation, b) it defines mysticism (i.e., authentic spirituality) by reference to one of its outcomes. Defining This is a common error in the literature.

[145]James Adam, *The Religious Teachers of Greece*, Gifford Lectures (New Jersey: Reference Book Publishers, 1965), https://www.giffordlectures.org/books/religious-teachers-greece.

[146]As for example found in the Yoga Sutras (i.e. union stitches) of Patanjali,

[147]Andrew Harvey, *Teachings of the Hindu Mystics*, Kindle (Boston: Shambhala Publications, 2001), https://amzn.to/2WQoduv.

[148]Yen, *Chan and Enlightenment*.

Huxley points out that the Vedic "though art that" is a perfect representation of the underlying unity of reality, and the experience we may have of this unity when we have a connection experience.[149] You also find the concept of ascension and union in Islamic spirituality, particularly the mystical Sufi variety. For example, the "Mi'rāj of Abu Yazīd" (the "Ascension of Abu Yazīd") is, despite its unfortunate patriarchy,[150] all about Abu Yazīd's experience of union with God.[151] Not surprisingly, you also find the concept of union and ascension in Christianity, particularly the mystical monastic variety, where ascension and final union is portrayed as either actual union with God,[152] or as "betrothal?" and "Divine/Spiritual Marriage."[153] As Xolani Kacela writes, "As the Holy Spirit descends upon us, ordinary experience is

---

[149] Aldous Huxley, *The Perennial Philosophy* (Canada: Random House Canada, 2014), https://amzn.to/2XGmQyM.

[150] It is important to recognize that almost all extant traditional spiritual doctrines are rooted in patriarchal experiences. This does not mean "men" are more capable of spiritual attainment. Rather, it is a result of toxic socialized ideologies that purport natural male dominance and hierarchy that excludes women or any "other" from access to spiritual knowledge and privilege. Authentic spirituality and connection has no binary gender.

[151] You can find a copy of this poem in Zaehner, *Hindu and Muslim Mysticism*.

[152] Climacus, *The Ladder of Divine Ascent*.

[153] St. Teresa of Avila, *The Way of Perfection*.

transformed into mystical experience, and we become one with the Spirit."[154]

There's more!

Evelyn Underhill, an Anglican mystic and pacifist writer, wrote a highly successful book on mysticism entitled *Mysticism* where she defines mysticism as "...*the art of union with Reality. The mystic is a person who has attained that union in greater or less degree; or who aims at and believes in such attainment*[155]. Underhill goes on:

> Broadly speaking, I understand it to be the expression of the innate tendency of the human spirit towards complete harmony with the transcendental order; whatever be the theological formula under which that order is understood. This tendency, in great mystics, gradually captures the whole field of consciousness; it dominates their life and, in the experience called "mystic union," attains its end. Whether that end be called the God of Christianity, the World-soul of Pantheism, the Absolute of Philosophy, the desire to attain it and the movement towards it--so long as this is a genuine life process and not an intellectual

---

[154] Xolani Kacela, "Being One with the Spirit: Dimensions of a Mystical Experience," *The Journal of Pastoral Care & Counseling* 60, no. 1–2 (Spr 2006): 85.

[155] Underhill, *Mysticism: A Study in the Nature and Development of Spiritual Consciousness*: emphasis added.

speculation--is the proper subject of mysticism. I believe this movement to represent the true line of development of the highest form of human consciousness.[156]

Finally, the notion of union with a higher Reality or Divine source is even represented in the secular world. Science Fiction Writer Arthur C. Clarke's book *Childhood's End*[157] is all about the transcendental evolution of humanity and its eventual connection/union with a higher source, or Overmind, as it is portrayed in the book.

As you can see, the idea of ascension and the gradual union that occurs as the process unwinds is a big topic of authentic spirituality. From the Yoga of the East to the monastic practices of the West, a lot of space is given over in the spiritual literature of this planet to outlining authentic spiritual practices that encourage connection and perfection of union. And note, it is not just theoretical discussion. Indeed, the spiritual literature of this planet is filled with **connection manuals** (manuals that teach how to connect), **ascension manuals** (manuals that provide guidance on the process of ascension and union), **alignment manuals** (manuals that teach one how to act properly), and so on. Sankaracharya's *Crest-Jewel of Wisdom*, for example, is a classic of Vedic spirituality. It offers extended guidance

---

[156]Underhill.

[157]Arthur C. Clarke, *Childhood's End* (New York: Del Rey, 1987).

on how to prepare one's self for connection.[158] Similarly, the Buddhist Eight Fold Path[159] is a shorthand manual on the establishment of **right thoughts**, **right actions**, and the **right environments** conducive towards connection and union. Finally, arguably, the Christian Ten Commandments lays the foundational structure for connection by focusing on non violence and emotionally safe spaces and relationships.

As with awakening and activation, the process of ascension and union can be experienced in both positive/Zenith and negative/Nadir ways. People can experience and even integrate bliss and joy, cosmic wonder, and deep revelation, but they can also experience **flooding**,[160] **ego explosion**,[161] **existential terrors**,[162] and other Nadir-type connection experiences that are difficult to integrate. Flooding, for example, can occur when an individual's thought process during connection are so overwhelming that the individual loses control and becomes "flooded" by thoughts and emotions so big, and moving so fast, that the bodily ego

---

[158] Adi Sankaracharya, *The Crest-Jewel of Wisdom: An LP Annotation* (Alberta: Lightning Path Press, 2019), https://datadump.lightningpath.org/annotations/Crest.Jewel.of.Wisdom-Shankara-Sosteric.pdf.

[159] Rahula, "The Noble Eightfold Path."

[160] http://spiritwiki.lightningpath.org/Flooding

[161] http://spiritwiki.lightningpath.org/Egoic_Explosion

[162] http://spiritwiki.lightningpath.org/Existential_Terrors

is simply incapable of processing "in the moment." Recall Cortright here:

> New and expanded states of consciousness [caused by connection] can overwhelm the ego. An infusion of powerful spiritual energies can flood the body and mind, fragmenting the structures of the self and temporarily incapacitating the person until they can be assimilated.[163]

What do you do if you are overwhelmed during an **ascension experience**? Deep breathing, a cold shower, a calm nature walk, and even rocking in a fetal position can help get you through the negative experience. Beyond these "trauma" measures, dealing with it will require psychological and emotional processing, spiritual re-education, sophisticated spiritually-focused therapy, and, in rare cases, even mental health assistance. Providing extended guidance is beyond the scope of this work, and there isn't much "out there" in the way of authentic and meaningful help, especially when dealing with the neurosis and psychosis that may result; but some work has been done on the issue. If you wish to explore more, Grof's "Spiritual Emergency"[164] may help. In the meantime, be proactive and work to

---

[163] "An Integral Approach to Spiritual Emergency.," *Guidance & Counseling* 15, no. 3 (2000): 12.

[164] Grof and Grof, *Spiritual Emergency: When Personal Transformation Becomes a Crises.*

establish right thought, right action, and right environment conducive and supportive of connection and union.

Summary

A lot more could be said and a lot more research has to be done on the four outcome measures of healing, awakening, activation, and ascension. In particular, how to overcome resistance, how to facilitate positive **connection experience**, how to deal with Nadir experiences, and how to approach and understand connection pathology. Pieces of relevant research in neurology, psychology, sociology, and even medicine are now beginning to appear, but scientists are really just at the start (more accurately restart) of inquiry. Hopefully at this point however you get a general sense of what authentic spirituality might mean, and a general notion how we might approach understanding and investigating the area.

With the ideas of authentic spirituality, connection, and connection outcomes under your belt, you have enough to be able to assess the authenticity of a spiritual path or practice. If a spirituality, religion, or practice leads you to connection experiences, and if these connection experiences lead to connection outcomes, then the spirituality or practice is likely authentic. However, just looking for connection experiences and connection outcomes is not enough. As I point out in an article entitled "Everyone Has a Connection Experience," connection experiences are not rare and they are not difficult to induce.[165] In fact, chances are that when you resolve nomenclature confusion and include Nadir experiences in the mix, just about everybody is going to have had at least one of these experiences at some point in their life, and probably more. The ease at which these experiences may be triggered means that coming up with practices that induce connection is probably not that hard, and it can probably happen just about anywhere, and under the influence of just about anyone with a basic understanding of the process. From Churches to nature resorts, from Osho led ashrams to Masonic lodges and "satanic" temples, the best-kept secret of connection is that it is very easy to accomplish.

Of course, the question that arises at this point is simple. Is an experience triggered by the teaching of a selfish satanic priest in a black ritual, an egoistic new age guru in an ashram surrounded by Rolls Royce limousines, or an exclusive invite-to-the-rich-only Masonic Lodge, the same as a connection experience led by a teacher like Christ, Suzuki, Eckhart, or Muhammad? Intuitively the answer would be no. Scientifically, there is minimal, if any, research which distinguishes between the types of connection experiences induced in a

---

[165]Sosteric, "Everybody Has a Connection Experience: Prevalence, Confusions, Interference, and Redefinition."

Masonic Lodge versus the types of connection experiences induced in a monastery devoted to human service, or a retreat devoted to yogic union, *but there are likely major differences.* As we saw briefly under the connection outcome of activation, most mystics emphasize ethical and moral action, service to the poor, ministering to the sick, or other self-less actions as prerequisites of authentic connection.[166] A connection experience arrived at in that sort of context is probably very different than a connection experience arrived at in a Mason's lodge surrounded by self-important business people.

Given that there are likely differences between the types of connection experiences and outcomes induced in Masonic lodges versus the types induced in temples led by selfless teachers, it seems reasonable to suggest that there is more to authentic spirituality than merely having a connection experience and experiencing one or more of the four connection outcomes. The question before us now is, what is that more?

In the final section of this book, we are going to look at additional factors which should be present in a spirituality if it is to be considered authentic. We may call these factors the **Seven Pillars of Authentic Spirituality**. These pillars are high standards, strict

---

[166] Christ's Sermon on the Mount is the classic example here. https://www.Biblegateway.com/passage/?search=Matthew+5-7&version=NIV

standards, and they must be present in any spirituality or spiritual practice in order for it to stake the claim that it is authentic. If the pillars of authentic spirituality are not present, the spiritual system and the person pimping the system are not authentic, period, end of sentence, closing paragraph, new chapter. If these pillars are not reflected in the actions of the gurus and the teachings of the masters of the path, my advice would be to avoid the teachings, avoid the teachers, and find a different path home.

Part Three: Seven Pillars of Authentic Spirituality

As noted in the previous unit of this book, healing, awakening, activation, and ascension are outcome measures you can use to assess whether the connection experiences you have, and the spiritual path you are following, is authentic or not. Most of the time, these experiences are positive; however, sometimes they can be negative, or have negative elements. Whether Zenith or Nadir, experiences of healing, awakening, activation, and ascension towards union are significant connection outcomes and should be present if a spirituality is to be counted as authentic.

Connection, connection experiences, and connection outcomes are important indicators of authentic spirituality, but by themselves, they are not enough to guarantee a path is authentic. This is because, despite propaganda to the contrary, connection experiences are not that hard to come by. Indeed, as pointed out in an article entitled "Everybody has a connection experience,"[167] people often have them spontaneously. Not only that, but connection experiences are easy to induce. Various **Connection**

---

[167]Sosteric, "Everybody Has a Connection Experience: Prevalence, Confusions, Interference, and Redefinition."

Techniques, like Transcendental Meditation (TM), Zen meditation, and so on, have been developed over the centuries that work to facilitate connection. In addition, individuals can use powerful **Connection Supplements**[168] to induce connection experience, either on their own or in "Shamanic" settings.

FYI, a connection supplement is a natural or artificial supplement like Cannabis, Psilocybin, Ayahuasca, LSD, and so on, that forces a connection between spiritual ego and bodily ego. As Bennet notes, connection supplements like cannabis have been used to facilitate connection for thousands of years.

Whether connection happens spontaneously or is induced by techniques or supplements is beside the point here. The point here is, connection is easy to come by and many people, even mentally ill people, can have them.

It is important to understand, connection experiences can be powerful and transformative, but they represent only brief hints of what is really possible when we persistently and consistently pursue union through connection practice. In other words, union between spiritual ego and bodily ego is not a binary "now you've done it" sort of thing. It is a process of continual improvement of connection. It requires more

---

[168] Chris Bennett, *Liber 420: Cannabis, Magickal Herbs and the Occult* (Walterville, OR: Trine Day, 2018).
http://spiritwiki.lightningpath.org/Connection_Supplements

than just a single "nirvana" experience or two, no matter how powerful and enlightening that single experience may be. As evidenced by the copious spiritual corpus of this planet, authentic progress on an authentic spiritual path requires good schools, good teachers, and lots of practice. Indeed, perfect union requires ongoing healing and connection practice, and ongoing effort to merge and unite. It requires spiritual, psychological, education, mental, emotional healing and training, as well as appropriate and supportive environments, and accurate and authentic **Connection Frameworks.**[169]

A connection framework is an organized training system designed to teach you how to connect. Every culture has its own established connection framework, which is more or less effective. Some examples that come to mind here are Zen Buddhism, Sufism (the "mystical" side of Islam), and Monastic Christianity (the mystical side of the Catholic Church). In addition, new connection frameworks pop up from time to time, like the Arica School of Oscar Ichazo,[170] as do "special interest" connection frameworks, like the connection framework provided by Freemasonry.

Do you really need a connection framework to help you connect? The answer is no. You can go about

---

[169] https://spiritwiki.lightningpath.org/Connection_Framework

[170] Dorothy De Christopher, "I Am the Root of a New Tradition," in *Interviews with Oscar Ichazo* (New York: Arica Institute Press, 1982), 129–54, https://amzn.to/2MOwleU.

connection on your own. You can learn how to open, control, and ground a connection without the help of a teacher or a connection framework. Zen Buddhists have a name for someone like that. They call it Jiriki (self-power), which is seeking enlightenment (read connection) through one's own effort and practice, and without outside assistance. However, sorting it all out on your own is a lot of work, it can take a long time, and, for reasons I'll go into at a later date, the process is prone to bias and error. You can make faster progress if you find good resources and a good teacher.

If you make the choice to find good resources and good teachers, then the next question is, what is a good resource? How do you find an authentic spiritual teacher or an authentic connection framework? Whose books do you read? Whose videos do you watch? Whose churches and temples do you attend? It sounds like an easy decision. However, it is not. Just walking into some spiritually inclined book store and picking up a book, going to a local established church, entering an esoteric temple, or selecting the guru with the most convincing **connection account**,[171] is not enough. Despite what we

---

[171] A connection account is somebody's account of their own connection experience. Connection accounts are peppered throughout the spiritual literature of this planet. Connection accounts always include a description of connection, and they usually include some indication of the connection outcomes that resulted. Sometimes, they may even indicate the connection supplement or connection practice that induced the connection experience, though since connection supplements are often illegal, this information is

might think, just because somebody has had a powerful connection experience or two doesn't make them suddenly liberated and enlightened. As noted in the previous section, connection outcomes are relatively easy to accomplish. What is more noteworthy, even those with serious mental illness can experience connection.[172] Not only that, connection experiences can be hard to interpret and easy to misunderstand, especially when filtered through unexamined bias. In other words, just because an individual has a connection experience, doesn't mean this person is instantly enlightened, liberated, emancipated, and capable of teaching others. Similarly, just because a connection framework purports to provide you with authentic spirituality, doesn't mean it does. From mental illness to cultural bias to just plain political malfeasance, there's a lot of spiritual nonsense out there and, consequently, a lot can get in the way of you finding a good path or a good teacher. It is far more problematic than you might think.

---

often left out. Connection outcomes are often taken as signs of spiritual legitimacy and spiritual wisdom, though of course, even mentally ill individuals can have them, and they can be easily falsified.

[172] The book "Memoirs of my Nervous Illness" is a fascinating account of a paranoid schizophrenic struggling to understand a problematic spiritual connection. Daniel Paul Schreber, *Memoirs of My Nervous Illness* (New York: NYRB Classics, 2000), https://amzn.to/2U8Se6Q.

Corrupted Connection Frameworks

xxx

These are provocative statements to be sure, especially considering most people have been trained to just accept spiritual "truths" without thought, from whatever source that has the audacity to claim authenticity. However, we can add substance to these statements by considering some extant connection frameworks which have been corrupted. There are examples down through the centuries of authentic connection frameworks being co-opted and corrupted by special interest groups with no real interest in authentic spiritual outcomes. One example that comes to mind here are the teachings of Zoroaster. Zoroaster was an ancient Persian mystic whose connection experiences, and the wisdom they purportedly proffered, were transmitted by word of mouth for several centuries before they were finally co-opted from the word of mouth record and written down by elite priests in ancient Sasanian courts, during the third century A.D.[173] Why did the elite write the teachings down? As pointed out in an article entitled "From Zoroaster to Star Wars, Jesus to Marx; The Science and Technology of Mass Human Behaviour,"[174] it was not because they wanted

---

[173]Mary Boyce, *Zoroastrians: Their Religious Beliefs and Practices* (Routledge, 2001).

[174]See Sosteric, "From Zoroaster to Star Wars, Jesus to Marx: The Science and Technology of Mass Human Behaviour."

people to connect and be empowered. After all, an empowered citizenry might overthrow lordly elites. Instead, the ancient priests used the Zoroastrian faith as a foundation upon which they created a spiritual ideology of submission and control that allowed them to suppress, manipulate, and incite the masses to violence and attack. This spiritual ideology was organized around what we would call **ideological nodes.**[175]

The ideological nodes developed by Sasanian priests are identified in the article, and we will not rehearse them here. However, as an example here, one of the more powerful nodes provided by Zoroastrianism is the notion of a cosmic fight between good and evil. The Zoroastrian faith purports a battle between cosmic forces of good and evil, personified as Ahura Mazda and Agra Mainu. This battle is a battle in which humans must pick a side. Humans pick a side and then fight the evil ones on the other side, sometimes to the death. Of course, it is always the other side that is evil. The ideology always encourages people to ignore their own vile behaviours, and focus on the perpetrator. Thus a crusading Knight or Jihadist is fighting for "good," even though they might massacre women and children in the process.

Elites use this ideology, and in particular the "good versus evil" node, to incite their populations to violence. All an elite agent has to do is convince their people that

---

[175]https://spiritwiki.lightningpath.org/Ideological_Node

some "other" population in another city-state or country is "evil," and their people will be primed for attack. You can see how these nodes would be useful not only for defence, but also for imperialist attack. If you can convince "your" people that "their" people are vile, evil, communist, atheist, rapist, satanic hordes, you can get your armies to attack. You can also see these nodes being used in contemporary global politics. Donald Trump, 45th president of the United States, is a master at using these nodes to weaponize individuals and groups and turn them against his enemies, like the press, or the "liberal" elite.

As you can see, this node, which is active even to do this day, exists not only in exoteric religion. It is also in Hollywood productions like Star Wars and every Marvel movie ever made.[176] It is particularly useful for any ruler, democratic or otherwise, who wants to get their hands on the resources of other beings and needs to use the people as a weapon of attack.

To be perfectly honest, since we don't have a record of the word of mouth teachings of Zoroaster, and since our only record of these teachings is what the Sasanian priests wrote down in the Gathas, we'll never know what Zoroaster actually had to say about things, so we'll never be able to argue with certainty that the Persian elites co-

---

[176] Mike Sosteric, "Star Wars Is a Religion That Primes Us for War and Violence," *The Conversation*, 2018, https://theconversation.com/star-wars-is-a-religion-that-primes-us-for-war-and-violence-89443.

opted a Zoroastrian connection framework to create an ideological frame for the manipulation of the masses; but, the fact that "good versus evil" is still used by world leaders today to justify imperialism and murder is a pretty strong argument that these nodes are in fact elite tools. There is less doubt about elite interference, however, when it comes to Christ and Catholicism, because there are written records (the Gospels) of Christ's activities, and we know these records were co-opted and edited by elite agents. As we discover when we actually read the New Testament, as I did while researching an article entitled "Rock and Roll Jesus,"[177] Christ was a populist revolutionary leader who was anti-hate and anti-establishment. He came out against hypocrisy and corruption and was wildly popular as a result. Because of his rapidly growing popularity, and because of his progressive message, he was a clear threat to the elites of the time. In the hopes of curtailing the impact of his teachings, the elites of the time had him assassinated. As outlined in the article, that didn't work. His assassination martyred him and ignited a connection wildfire. People were talking about it, writing about it, and organically spreading the word far and wide. To stop the revolution from spreading, the elites had to do more than simply assassinate the leader.

---

[177]Sosteric, "Rethinking the Origins and Purpose of Religion: Jesus, Constantine, and the Containment of Global Revolution."

Their solution, in addition to persecution, was to co-opt the original teachings. The watershed moment came at the Synod of Hippo when then emperor Constantine got together with a bunch of elite Catholic bishops and handpicked what we may presume to be the twenty-seven least radical, most conservative, "safest" Christian texts that were around at the time. The elite Bishops put these twenty-seven safe (for them) texts together into what they called the New Testament Bible.[178] Then, they tossed the rest away and presented this elite-approved canon to hungry Christians as the only written accounts that they could read.[179] In this way, elites controlled what future generations would know about the personality and activities of Christ.

Now, the faithful might like to think, perhaps because it preserves their spiritual investment and saves them some face, that the activities of the emperor and his cadre of elite bishops were benign. However,

---

[178] Although note that some of the "Lost Gospels" have been rediscovered. These are presented in the Nag Hamadi library. James M. Robinson, *The Nag Hammadi Library: The Definitive New Translation of the Gnostic Scriptures*, Third (San Francisco: Harper, 1988).

[179] As Bernard Starr notes, "... the Council of Hippo sanctioned 27 books for the New Testament in 393 C.E. Four years later the Council of Cartage confirmed the same 27 books as the authoritative Scriptures of the Church. Bernard Starr, "Why Christians Were Denied Access to Their Bible for 1,000 Years," *Huffpost Religion*, July 20, 2013.

subsequent actions of the Church highlight their true motivation, which was to suppress the revolutionary texts.

One thing that the elites in the Catholic Church did, in addition to their purge of the written record, was to hide and suppress even the cannon they had chosen away. To be clear, they hid the Bible that they created away in monasteries, kept it in a language few people at the time could read, and prevented the peasants from ever having access to it. As Bernard Starr notes, "the Church actually discouraged[180] the populace from reading the Bible on their own — a policy that intensified through the Middle Ages."[181] They prohibited the "laity" from having access to the New Testament, they burned any copies that existed outside the Church, they even burned people at the stake who tried to distribute and/or translate the Bible! In 1536, William Tyndale was strangled and burned by the Catholic Church for having the unmitigated, revolutionary,

---

[180] Starr uses the word "discouraged," but as he himself points out, the Church actually executed people for spreading the word. This is a level above mere "discouragement." It is active suppression of spiritual teachings. Bernard Starr, *Jesus Uncensored: Restoring the Authentic Jew* (OmniHouse Publishing, 2013).

[181] Bernard Starr, "Why Christians Were Denied Access to Their Bible for 1,000 Years."

Also check out this web page http://www.aloha.net/~mikesch/banned.htm. It lists documentary evidence of a centuries long attempt by members of the elite to prevent the public from accessing the Bible.

heretical gall of having the Latin Bible translated and printed in English so that the people could read it directly.[182]

Another thing the elites did that speaks to their true motivation, in addition to purging the literature and hiding the remaining away, was mercilessly edit it once it was in their control. The truth is, the Bible you read today is not the Bible that was created at the council of Hippo. The Bible of today is a heavily edited version of the original New Testament. Even conservative Christian scholars admit the Bible has been edited thousands of times,[183] and this is not insignificant. Even if one could argue that the edits were mostly grammar and punctuation edits, this is enough to seriously call into question the activities of the elite church. Even a single punctuation mark can dramatically change the meaning of a sentence! Consider the following example:

---

[182] For a brief overview of what happened, see the Christianity.com article "Translator William Tyndale Strangled and Burned," Christianity.Com, http://www.christianity.com/church/church-history/timeline/1501-1600/translator-william-tyndale-strangled-and-burned-11629961.html. If you read that version note how obstinate Tyndale was and how mad the Church got at him.

[183] Bart D. Ehrman, *Misquoting Jesus: The Story Behind Who Changed the Bible and Why* (Harper One, 2007); *Lost Scriptures* (New York: Oxford University Press, 2003).

> A woman without her man is nothing
> A woman: without her, man is nothing.

Only two punctuation marks are changed, yet the meaning of the sentence is reversed. One of the above statements is empowering to women, and the other beats her down. When you remember the Bible has been edited thousands of times by the Church, this is shocking. If even a colon and a comma can change the meaning of a sentence, you can imagine the modifications that become possible when you have hundreds of years to privately edit "the Word."

At this point, a couple of questions may be lingering. The first question that may linger is, if the teachings of Christ were such a threat, why not simply erase the books altogether? The answer is simply that it was too late. By the time the elites got around to co-opting the corpus, his teaching had already spread far enough that any attempt to simply erase them would likely have led to a violent uprising.[184] Assassination hadn't stopped the revolutionary message from spreading, it just made it worse; trying to burn all the accounts wouldn't do it either. It would probably just make it worse.

---

[184] Sosteric, "Rethinking the Origins and Purpose of Religion: Jesus, Constantine, and the Containment of Global Revolution."

Another question that may linger at this point is about the actual power of the Christ's life, and his teachings. Was his life and work really a threat? Did the elites really put in centuries of effort trying to suppress the Gospels for fear of the revolution they might insight? It sounds like magical thinking, as I'm sure Richard Dawkins would agree, but consider the story of Spanish conquistador Bartolome de las Casas. Bartolome de las Casas was a member of the 16h century Spanish elite. He was directly involved in the colonization of Hispaniola and Cuba. As Fiske notes of the repressive practices of the colonizers:

> Indians were slaughtered by the hundreds, burned alive, impaled on sharp stakes, torn to pieces by blood-hounds. In retaliation for the murder of a Spaniard, it was thought proper to call up fifty or sixty Indians and chop off their hands. Little children were flung into the water to drown with less concern than if they had been puppies. In the mingling of sacred ideas with the sheerest devilry, there was a grotesqueness fit for the pencil of Dore. Once, "in honour and reverence of Christ and his twelve Apostles," they hanged thirteen Indians in a row at such a height that their toes could just touch the ground and then pricked them to death with their sword-points, taking care not to kill them quickly. At another time, when some old

reprobate was broiling half a dozen Hideout Indians in a kind of cradle suspended over a slow fire, their shrieks awoke the Spanish captain who, in a neighboring hut, was taking his afternoon nap and he called out testily to the man to despatch those wretches at once and stop their noise. But this demon, determined not to be baulked of his enjoyment, only gagged the poor creatures.[185]

Las Casas was considered one of the worst of the worst, a monster by any account, until one day while in Cuba, while reading from a Church pulpit, he read the following words from the Bible:

The Most High is not pleased with the offerings of the wicked: neither is he pacified for sin by the multitude of sacrifices. The bread of the needy is their life; he that defraudeth him thereof is a man of blood. He that taketh away his neighbors' living slayeth him; and he that defraudeth the laborer of his hire is a shedder of blood (Sira 34: 21-23).

Upon reading these words, Las Casas had a classic connection experience, and was instantly transformed by it. Fiske provides an account of the dramatic awakening.[186]

---

[185] John Fiske, *The Historical Writings of John Fiske: The Discovery of America*, 12 vols., vol. 3(New York: Houghton Mifflin, 1902).

[186] Fiske, *The Historical Writings of John Fiske: The Discovery of America*.

As he read these words, a light from heaven seemed to shine upon Las Casas. The scales fell from his eyes. He saw that the system of slavery was wrong in principle. The question whether you treated your slaves harshly or kindly did not go to the root of the matter. As soon as you took from the laborer his wages, the deadly sin was committed; the monstrous evil was inaugurated. There must be a stop put to this, said Las Casas. We have started wrong. Here, are vast countries which the Holy Church has given to the Spaniards in trust, that the heathen may be civilized and brought into the fold of Christ; and we have begun by making Hispaniola a hell. This thing must not be suffered to grow with the growth of Spanish conquest. There was but one remedy. The axe must be put to the root of the tree. Slavery must be abolished .

Following his transformative experience, Las Casas gave up his slaves, went into the pulpit, and preached against the practice. He sold his worldly goods and went to visit the King of Spain, the Bishop Fonesca, and others. He became politically active and was a key figure and major influence not only in advocating against slavery, but in advocating for the idea that the slaves were human and had souls. Eventually, he went on to write a rather disturbing book on Spanish treatment of slaves where he provides a first-hand account of a horrific genocide that left Hispaniola a ruinous and desolate waste.[187]

You can see the threat represented by even the watered-down Bible the elites provided. It was so powerful, even a top member of the one percent could be instantly transformed by simply reading the words. No wonder the Catholic patriarchs did not want the masses reading it. No wonder some people were willing to risk persecution and immolation (e.g., William Tyndale) just to get the Bible into the hands of the people.

As we know, the efforts of the Church to suppress even the watered-down and edited accounts of Christ's life eventually, with the creation of the printing press, collapsed. After that, it was no longer possible to keep the Bible out of the hands of the masses. This didn't mean the Church gave up, however. In an ongoing effort to control access to the Bible, they organized Christian worship into Sunday masses and required the faithful to listen to a Catholic functionary (a priest) read and interpret out-of-context snippets of the Bible for them. I know of no sociological research comparing what the priests say in their Sunday services, with what is actually in the Bible; however, as a child, I did attend church regularly and I know a) the priests never talked about

---

[187] If you are interested in Las Casas first-hand account and condemnation, you can read the book. It is available from Project Gutenberg at http://www.gutenberg.org/ebooks/20321. Bartolome de las Casas, *A Brief Account of the Destruction of the Indies*.

connection or connection experience and b) they never spoke of the revolutionary content of Christ's teachings, or his revolutionary example. Taking quotes out of context, they spun the teachings and took both connection and revolution out. Instead, they portrayed Christ as a meek and passive Sheppard of sheeple, giving deference to a patriarchal and "godly" authority.

If you recall from the previous section of this book, awakening and activation are common connection outcomes. If you understand the exoteric Church represents world elites and not the interests of the people, you can understand why the Church would suppress, sanitize, and spin accounts of Christ's life into their opposite. You can also understand the problem spiritual seekers have. The Church will no doubt claim to provide an authentic avenue for human spiritual experience and practice, but does it really? For all the reasons outlined so far, at least when it comes to exoteric and non-monastic aspects of Christianity, the answer is no; but you can decide for yourself.

When it comes to assessing the authenticity of exoteric spirituality, in my view, we can stop on the absence of a concern with connection experience. However, there are others aspects of Christianity that arguably retain concern with connection experience. There is a place in the Christian fabric for spiritual experience. Monk and nuns in the Christian mystical tradition monastic traditions of Christianity speak of connection experience (which they call union with God, or a divine marriage) and even provide advice on how to attain it. The book *The Ladder of Divine Ascent*[188] by 6th century Christian mystic John Climacus is an example in this regard, as are the works of St. Teresa of Avila.[189] And, as pointed out earlier, activation is a component of Christian mystical tradition.[190] There are also aspects of Christianity that retain the revolutionary character of the original teachings, for example, Liberation Theology. Finally, there are Christian "esoteric" traditions[191] that do overtly claim, at least to their members, that they provide an authentic connection framework. Freemasonry is one example of that. Freemasonry is definitely a connection framework, since Freemasons use words and images that clearly indicate a concern with connection and union. Just do an online image search for "Masonic tracing board" and you will see ladders of ascent to starry realms of higher awareness

---

[188] Climacus, *The Ladder of Divine Ascent*.

[189] St. Teresa of Avila, *The Way of Perfection*; St. Teresa of Avila, *Interior Castle*, Kindle (New York: Dover Publications, 2007), https://amzn.to/2GpC7NG.

[190] Harvey, *Teachings of the Christian Mystics*.

[191] An esoteric tradition is an institutionalized, but "secret," spiritual tradition. Esoteric traditions provide spiritual knowledge outside of and hidden from the mainstream. Esoteric traditions are generally exclusive, often male-only, invite-only affairs open only to a "chosen few." You have to be invited into the fold to be a Freemason, for example. Members are treated to "secret" knowledge available only to membership.

and consciousness. As one Mason says, "...we must climb the steps to achieve a type of gnosis which comes with the achievement of...an inseparable union."[192] This is classic connection talk.

Do Christian monastic traditions, Liberation Theology, Freemasonry, and so on, qualify as authentic connection frameworks? If our only measure was whether or not these frameworks provided a path towards connection experience, the answer would be yes, and we could stop right here. However, it is likely more complicated than that. In my view, Christian monastic traditions represent a containment of connection experience. Monastic traditions are not open traditions. Their members are cloistered, confined, and subject to Clerical authority. For example, in *The Way of Perfection*, St. Teresa of Avila repeatedly appeals to and confirms her submission to the authority of the Church Bishops.[193] It is an open question how much authenticity is retained within an institutional fabric (i.e. Christianity) that is hostile to certain connection outcomes.

As for Freemasonry, as discussed in the article "The Sociology of Tarot," these are elite organizations with elite agendas.[194] They use the cover of esoteric

---

[192] Gregory B. Stewart, *Fellow of the Craft; A Treatise on the Second Degree of Freemasonry* (FMI Publishing, 2015), 40.

[193] St. Teresa of Avila, *The Way of Perfection*.

[194] Sosteric, "A Sociology of Tarot."

spirituality to bend and twist human spirituality in the service of their economic and political interests. The clear affiliation of Freemasonry with economic elites and their creation of spiritual propaganda in the form of the Western Tarot deck belie any claims they might make concerning the authenticity of their tradition.

Uneducated, Biased and Mentally Ill Gurus

If Christian monastic traditions represent a sanitized and contained mysticism, and if Freemasonry and other esoteric organizations represent elite manipulation of human spirituality, then it is doubtful you can rely on the presence of connection experience and connection outcome to assess authenticity.

Unfortunately, the problem of assessing the authenticity of a spirituality goes beyond the institutional component of human spirituality. Even if you do find a relatively pure representation of spiritual truths about connection, for example, in a tradition like Zen Buddhism, there is still the issue of who teaches the framework. If you follow a connection framework, your interface with that framework is always at least partially mediated by another human being who has written a book or who teaches in an ashram, monastery, or whatever. Teachers who teach spiritual traditions are human and can introduce biases, confusions, and other problems which can corrupt and skew even a relatively pure connection framework.

One problem we often find is simply naive and confused teachers. The problem is that when it comes to "mystical" experience, people can claim to be experienced sojourners, spiritual teachers, and gurus despite having had little or no training or connection experience. Often all that is required for a person to don the Mantle of Spiritual Authority is that a person have a single spiritual experience or two and *boom*, suddenly they believe themselves to be a fully qualified spiritual teacher capable of proselytizing about the deepest mystical (read connection) issues. This would be kind of like a skier without medical training successfully relocating a dislocated shoulder, and then presuming that this makes them a fully trained doctor. They may have latent skill, but that's as far as it goes.

This tendency for **naive initiates** to instantly turn on as fully qualified spiritual teachers despite the fact they've only had a single experience is a problem that occurs frequently enough. Just scan the YouTube airways. It happens because connection experiences are intoxicating. They come quite easily, they can be quite powerful, and even a single experience can leave you with a deep sense of gnosis and enlightenment. Unfortunately, the powerful experience can fool an individual into thinking they have already reached their goal and that they are qualified to proselytize, even when they are merely naive, have only started their journey, or are deeply confused.[195] It is well-known in the psychological literature on mystical experience that people struggle with their "ineffable" "noetic" initial experiences. They struggle to understand. Even when they themselves understand, they still struggle to put their experiences into words. Not that you need to be an Arhat Buddha[196] just to talk about and research connection, but you do have to be aware that people struggle to understand and explain, and they are not always aware of their own struggle. In fact, sometimes, like the lucky skier who successfully set a bone, they project experience and wisdom even when they are still quite naive.

The tendency for naive initiates to adopt a mantle of authority is more common than you might think. For example, Canadian medical doctor Richard Bucke wrote a classic text on connection experience entitled *Cosmic Consciousness: A Study in the Evolution of the Human Mind*,[197] despite the fact that he only ever had one connection experience, and not a very impressive one at that. The book is not without merit. At the same time,

---

[195] This is a problem noted in by Sufi 'Ala' al-Dawla Simnan in the book *The Clarification of the Virtue of People of Divine Knowledge (d. 1336)*, in Carl W. Ernst, *Teachings of Sufism* (Boston: Shambhala, 1999).

[196] In Theravada Buddhism, an Arhat is an individual who has achieved "nirvana," or someone who can maintain connection on a relatively permanent bases.

[197] Bucke, *Cosmic Consciousness: A Study in the Evolution of the Human Mind*.

however, it was written by a naive initiate with only one connection experience. A more sophisticated, critical, and informed reading may ultimately reveal it lacks breadth and depth.

Obviously, looking directly at a solar eclipse doesn't instantly make you a nuclear physicist. Similarly, a single "cosmic" experience doesn't make you a trained and healthy Bodhisattva, capable of teaching the world.[198] In fact, a single experience, even a dozen, cannot guarantee clarity of vision, purity of intent, pedagogical sophistication, or even mental health. The truth is, people can have a connection experience, or even ten, and still be confused, greedy, power-hungry, and even mentally ill.

A good example of confusion is the case of *Carlos Castaneda*. Castaneda was a mystical anthropologist who claimed to have shamanic style connection experiences and who published several successful books touting the

---

[198] It takes a lot to develop authentic spirituality to the point where it can be presented to the world and it takes more than just knowledge to be able to teach it properly. Additional skill and training goes into writing and teaching connection. The extra effort that goes into being a "connection" teacher is probably why traditional spiritualties reserve their highest status positions to teachers who come to teach the masses, like "saviours," "prophets," "buddhi," "brahmani," and so on. There is a discussion of this by 'Ala' al-Dawla Simnani where he attempts to distinguish an experience teacher from one without the necessary depth of knowledge and virtue. See *The Clarification of the Virtue of People of Divine Knowledge*. 'Ala' al-Dawla Simnani (d. 1336), excerpted in *Ernst, Teachings of Sufism*..

"Yaqui Way of Knowledge."[199] As it turns out, however, he made most of his stuff up.[200] He may have had authentic connection experiences, in fact he probably did, but for whatever reason (mental health, ego, laziness, the need to feel special, his own confusion, etc.), he stepped out of bounds, failed to represent them in an authentic and rigorous fashion, and may have in fact made a large portion of his "teachings" up. Castaneda sounds authentic and real, to someone who doesn't know better. However, anybody who thinks Castaneda's Yaqui teachings are authentic will waste time on spiritual vapour, will be confused by the meaningless conceptualizations, and will be frustrated in their attempts to find authentic spirituality and authentic connection. Sadly and unfortunately, the publisher of his works, Simon and Schuster, continues to misrepresent the corpus as non-fiction,[201] and people continue to go to Carlos Castaneda seeking authentic spiritual knowledge. Shockingly, I even had a senior academic colleague recommend me to Carlos Castaneda once.

Confusion and misrepresentation are not the only "sins" of the initiatory naive. Money and power play a

---

[199] Carlos Castaneda, *The Teachings of Don Juan: A Yaqui Way of Knowledge, 40th Anniversary Edition* (New York: Washington Square Press, 1996).

[200] Marshall, "The Dark Legacy of Carlos Castaneda."

[201] Perhaps because profit is more important than truth, or perhaps because they are participating in the confusion and misdirection.

big role as well. There are well-known instances of "spiritual" teachers motivated by little more than a venal desire to line their pockets and dominate others. Being a spiritual teacher, especially one who claims to have had connection experiences, carries with it a certain amount of "mystical" status and prestige, and this status and prestige can easily be translated into respect, book sales, subscription fees, and so on. Of course, there is nothing intrinsically wrong with money, power, status, and respect, but if these things become the primary motivations for teaching an authentic spirituality, the authenticity can be jeopardized. The basic problem is this: someone who is motivated by money and power will, even if they truly understand the scholarship and experience of connection, shape and distort their teachings in a way that supports their enrichment and empowerment at the expense of authentic teaching. They will lock seekers into complicated hierarchies, engage in manipulative and unethical practices, and charge hundreds of thousand of dollars to unlock advanced content.[202] Each new level of "attainment," each impotent step towards spiritual enlightenment (and it must be impotent because if you successfully connect someone, there is no reason for them to keep handing over their money) brings additional and

---

[202]Jethro Nededog, "How Scientology Costs Members up to Millions of Dollars, According to Leah Remini's Show," Business Insider, 2016, https://www.businessinsider.com/scientology-costs-leah-remini-recap-episode-3-2016-12.

sometimes obscene expense, which goes on to fund boats and Rolls Royces, but which ultimately only the rich, or those willing to sell their homes and possessions, can afford. Regardless of how authentic the original source of a teaching may be, when money, status, and power are the goal, money, status, and power become the focus, and all manner of manipulative and unethical practices may be engaged in, in order to reach the venal goal.[203]

Losing your money and all your possessions to some questionable spiritual hack is unfortunate, but it is hardly the most significant loss you can face, especially when mental illness is involved. Consider Jonestown in Guyana in 1978 where 918 otherwise intelligent, progressive, and educated people drank cyanide-laced cool-aid at the behest of their spiritual "father," Jim Jones. Jim Jones was clearly mentally ill. There were obvious warning signs of this right from the start, but victims and survivors blithely ignored these warnings, not because they were stupid, but because they were desperately seeking spiritual, political, and social authenticity in a chaotic and changing world, and because Jim Jones seemed, at least at the start, to provide that authenticity. By survivor accounts, Jones

---

[203]Russell Miller, *Bare-Faced Messiah: The True Story of L. Ron Hubbard* (London: Silvertail Books, 2015), https://amzn.to/2ESbMI5. For an example, see Jenna Miscavige Hill, "Beyond Belief: My Secret Life Inside Scientology and My Harrowing Escape EBook: Jenna Miscavige Hill, Lisa Pulitzer: Kindle Store," 2013, https://amzn.to/2W796kl.

started out a seemingly awake, activated, spiritually sophisticated, powerful, progressive, egalitarian, socialist leader seeking to build a utopian society free of inequality and racism.[204] In their desperation to realize this promised authenticity, they ignored warning signs and became trapped in a descending spiral of violence, paranoia, and indoctrination, with absolutely disastrous results.

Between the venal enterprises of publisher supported spiritual charlatans and the murderous activities of cult leaders like Jim Jones lies a vast and turbulent ocean of spiritually naive, confused, villainous, and mentally ill actors who talk about everything from corrupted filaments of God to cosmic shape-shifting lizards and cosmic intergalactic conspiracies. Sometimes, as in the case of paranoid schizophrenic Daniel Paul Schreber,[205] the connection and the mental illness are obvious. At other times, the mental illness is obscured behind a patina of charisma, reason, intelligence, and superficial authenticity which makes it hard for some to distinguish and discern. Such is the case of David Icke who seems to have had authentic connection experiences, but whose connection

---

[204]Laura Johnston Kohl, *Jonestown Survivor* (iUniverse, 2010), https://amzn.to/2WJFtoK; Deborah Layton, *Seductive Poison* (New York: Anchor Books, 2010), https://amzn.to/2wxOse4.

[205]Schreber, *Memoirs of My Nervous Illness*.

experiences are filtered through a paranoid and racist intellectual and emotional framework.[206]

The question for the person interested in authentic spirituality at this point is, how do you tell the difference between someone who has had many connection experiences and who has spent time healing their damage, establishing mental health, and integrating and grounding their experience, from someone who is naive, confused, venally motivated, and possibly mentally ill? It is an important question not only because following along behind a half-cocked paranoid schizophrenic messiah whose only interest is money and power probably won't lead to anywhere authentic, but because sometimes, lives are at stake.

Answering the question is a bit of challenge, and it is a challenge we cannot ignore. As my partner and I argue in "The Seven Essential Needs,"[207] humans have powerful, and probably biologically rooted, spiritual needs for actualization of, and connection to, Self. These needs can no more be extinguished than you can extinguish our need for nutritious food and water. But just like a corporation can divert your need for nutritious food to "satisfy" you with processed junk, so to can corporations, hucksters, charlatans, and the elite's

---

[206]Michael Barkun, *A Culture of Conspiracy: Apocalyptic Visions in Contemporary America* (California: University of California Press, n.d.); Abad-Santos, "Lizard People."

[207]Mike Sosteric and Gina Ratkovic, "Seven Essential Needs," 2018, https://www.academia.edu/38114100/The_Seven_Essential_Needs.

actors divert you down confusing and impotent pathways. We cannot ignore these spiritual needs and we cannot ignore the diversions that occur. We must raise the level of discourse and find ways to positively meet them, otherwise inauthentic traditions and mentally ill gurus will continue to ruin our days.

So, to return to the question, if the presence of connection experiences and connection outcomes are not enough to tell an authentic connection framework from an inauthentic framework, what else do we need? Well, if you want to increase your chances of finding an authentic connection framework and a knowledgeable teacher, you look, in addition to the presence of outcome measures, for the *Seven Pillars of Authentic Spirituality*. If you want to tell whether a connection framework, church, temple, priest, spiritual teacher, guru, evangelist, or whomever, is representing an authentic path, look for the Seven Pillars of Authentic Spirituality. Presence of all the Seven Pillars is a strong indication that the spirituality being represented is authentic, pure, and not corrupted, colonized, or represented in confused or inauthentic ways. Absence of a single one is a red flag and clear invitation to get out.

And just what are the seven pillars of authentic spirituality? Linking back to our earlier discussion, the seven pillars of authentic spirituality are like the engineering standards that professional engineers use when they set about to build their safe bridges.

Professional engineering standards are the ways of thinking about things, the procedures, the rules, and the guidelines that help engineers build solid and safe bridges. Likewise, the seven pillars are the standards upon which we can assess whether or not a spiritual tradition or spiritual teacher is authentic or not, and upon which we can build authentic, safe, spiritualties. When these seven pillars are present, you can be more confident that the path you are on, the person you are listening to, the screen you are connected with, or whatever, is providing authentic healing and connection guidance. When applied correctly, these pillars help you identify hucksters, pretenders, mentally ill gurus, and corrupted or ineffective systems of spirituality and thought, thereby saving you time, energy, confusion, and maybe even your life. If you find even one of the following pillars absent, *caveat emptor* applies.

We are going to move on to a discussion of these seven pillars in a moment. Before we do that, however, a few comments are in order.

First off, be clear, these pillars are not outcome measures as defined in the previous section of this book. That is, these are not things that happen to you as a consequence of connection. Rather, they are the things that you should look for to be present when "shopping around" for a path, a school, or a teacher that purports to offer connection guidance and human development. Think of these seven pillars as guideposts or markers, like fluorescent tags on a tree, that show you the way, even when it is dark and you are confused. If you are following a path of spirituality or human development, if a book you are reading or a teacher you are listening to does not present with all these pillars, chances are they are not fully authenticate.

Second, understand, even though these pillars are offered as guideposts and way signs, they are not intended as final statements on the nature of authentic spirituality or systems of human development. These pillars are not intended to end discussion and lay down final commandments. These pillars are provided to orient you to the idea of authentic spirituality and get you started on critically discerning psychological and spiritual practices. They are intended to initiate a much-needed discussion and dialogue on what counts as authentic spirituality. We certainly need a dialogue on what counts for accurate, professional, meaningful, and authentic spirituality, because authentic connection has profound implications for human health and well-being. It might even be implicated, as some suggest,[208] and as we tend to agree, in saving the planet. We need to open a discussion and raise the bar on what counts as valid, reliable, and authentic spiritual and psychological practice. If we do not do this, then we risk seeing ourselves and the people we love led down paths of

---

[208] Harvey, *Teachings of the Christian Mystics*.

sleepy disconnection that sicken and dis-empower rather than heal, awaken, activate, and unite.

Who really wants that?

And besides, in a world characterized by powerful technologies of death and enslavement, looming political and economic crises, and life-ending ecological catastrophe, we really cannot continue to brook half-baked spirituality, half-cocked gurus, and twisted and corrupted offerings. If our world collapses because we can't get people properly healed and connected, we are all doomed. We need to move forward and we need to move forward now.

Finally, third, be aware, there is a theory behind why these pillars are important and it has to do with the nature of the Consciousness that we connect to. I won't go into detail about the nature of this Consciousness here except to repeat what I have said already, and which all mystics will agree with, is that Consciousness is characterized by awareness, compassion, bliss, love, and vast intelligence. If awareness, compassion, bliss, love, intelligence are not reflected in the actual teachings and practices of the path or the guru, if you find them exclusionary, mean, bitter, passive-aggressive, judgmental, irresponsible, stupid, ungrounded, and dis-empowering, you have reasonable cause for suspicion and very good reason to question the authenticity and sincerity of the guru, path, or tradition.

With all that said, it is now time to have a brief look at the Seven Pillars of Authentic Spirituality.

1. Accessible and Inclusive

The first pillar of authentic spirituality is accessibility and inclusivity. In the early stages of exploration, when you are just getting your footing on a path of spiritual/human development, when you are just starting to read and evaluate a new spiritual author or guru, whatever path you are considering, should be accessibility and inclusivity.

What do accessibility and inclusivity mean? Put together, they mean that the path should be open to all. It means that there should be no exclusions. It means that nobody should be left out or "left behind" for any reason. This includes any exclusions based on skin colour, ethnicity, age, genetics, gender, income, or any other superficial criteria, no matter what. Neither should there be one set of rules and expectations for one group, and a different set for another group. There should be no inner circles or secret chambers, and power and privilege should not be available only to a chosen a few.

How does a spirituality achieve accessibility and inclusivity? Obviously, it has to be open to the public, and it has to be financially accessible to everyone. If you have to be invited in, like for example with Freemasonry and other secret boys clubs, if you have to engage in secret rituals to advance in a hierarchy, think twice. Also, consider the financial cost. There is nothing wrong with paying for services, but, at the same time, the fees have to be reasonable and there should always be an avenue in for those who cannot afford. It should never cost you your life savings and you should never be required to donate your house and other assets. If you are being asked to give more than what a resource or service is fairly worth, move on.

Also note, accessibility and inclusivity are about more than throwing wide the door and letting people through. In order for a spirituality to be accessible and inclusive, the door needs to be wide open and the teachings you find inside need to be clear and easy to understand. This should be obvious. If a spirituality is full of complicated jargon, esoteric verbiage, and pompous prognostication, what I, tongue in cheek, call EPMO, or Egotistical, Polly-syllabic, Multi-Metaphoric, Obfuscation,[209] it won't be accessible and inclusive. The goal of authentic spirituality is to develop a system that can enlighten and connect everybody. The only way to do that is to make things as simple and accessible as possible. You should not have to be a rocket scientist or a rabbinical rabbi to understand awakening, activation, connection, or the deep truths of creation. If you do, then something is askew. Despite what some people might say, obtuse and esoteric complexity does not represent valid spirituality. EPMO is a simple recipe for

---

[209] https://spiritwiki.lightningpath.org/EPMO

hierarchy, control, and exclusion. People who offer complex jargon as spiritual knowledge have one goal and one goal only, to exclude some people from their club.

The stipulation that authentic spirituality should communicate and be accessible applies not only to the meaning of things, it also extends to the interpretation of things. There should be no ambiguity in the teachings of an authentic path. Likewise, there should be no doubt and confusion. You should know what things mean, period.[210]

Clear, precise, grounded and easy to understand teachings are important. Clarity and precision remove barriers to inclusion, while ambiguity and confusion raise barriers. If you cannot understand things, you are immediately on the outside. What is worse, ambiguity and confusion allow for hierarchy and domination to emerge. Lack of clarity and precision allows for the development of distinctions between those who "know" and are "worthy," and those who do not know and are unworthy. It also facilitates massive global division where some people, some sects, some denominations, some clubs, some nations, some "races," may feel they

---

[210] To be sure, more advanced discussions might pose pedagogical challenges for those just starting on the path. That is, if you are new to the path and you do not know the concepts and ideas, you might have trouble understanding at first, and you might have learning to do. In the end, however, if you learn the concepts and ideas, the meanings should be clear and you should be able to understand and agree. When you cannot pin the meaning of spiritual texts down precisely, something is terribly wrong.

are superior and have the "right" interpretation, while others do not. When people start thinking that they are the only ones with the truth, or the only ones who can understand, the ground becomes fertile for the development of hierarchy, exclusion, and even violence.

Clarity and precision contribute to accessibility and inclusion, and help avoid the development of hierarchies and violence, and so they are important. The most important reason we need clarity and precision, however, is so we can judge for ourselves. If we are going to be able to assess a spirituality, spiritual practice, or spiritual teacher, if we are going to rely on our own thoughts and not the authority of someone else, we need clarity and precision. If a spirituality is confusing, if the concepts are messy and unclear, if you have to dig through multiple dusty volumes filled brimming over with obtuse and contorted EPMO, how can you tell if your path is authentic or the priest or guru knows what they are talking about? The answer is, you cannot. If a spirituality is filled with confusing and convoluted verbiage, if concepts are poorly specified and set out, and if it is all too complex and confusing to sort out, you will not be able to assess for yourself. Thus, in the interests of accessibility and personal discernment, spirituality and the concepts and ideas that make it up should be clear and precise. Excuses, like the common excuse that it is impossible to describe the luminous, otherworldly realities with any degree of accuracy, that it is impossible to be scientific and precise, or that "the plan" is mysterious and ineffable, do not apply. Concise, accurate, and accessible definitions that leave no space for misunderstanding and exclusion are an absolute prerequisite for building an authentic, accessible, and inclusive spirituality.

If you find that teachings are not accessible to certain groups, classes, ethnicities, or genders, if you find there are secret "inner chambers" and that only a few may enter, if people are excluded or put down in any way and for any reason whatsoever, then the path you are following is not authentic, period. If accessibility and inclusivity are not written into the very core of the teachings, you are not building, nor are you following, an authentic spiritual path.

Given this theoretical emphasis on accessibility, a reasonable question now would be to ask whether or not an emphasis on accessibility and inclusion is present in authentic spirituality traditions? It is something that is discussed and values? The answer is, yes. Gandhi, for example, was all about including everybody, especially the Hindu untouchable caste.[211] He had a particular emphasis on removing class distinctions and treating everybody on the same level. You find the same emphasis on accessibility and inclusion in the biography

---

[211]Mohandas Karamchand Gandhi, *Gandhi: An Autobiography*, trans. Mahadev Desai (Green Reader Publications, n.d.), https://amzn.to/2WnIbjB.

of Jesus Christ, who rejected elite culture and walked amongst and taught the poor and disenfranchised. This inclusivity continued in the years following his assassination. For example, 1 Corinthians 14: 6-12 specifically rejects speaking in tongues (an early form of EPMO?) because it confused people. Instead, it admonishes Christian to be clear and precise in their communications.

You also find this emphasis extended to the work of, for example, Christian mystics. The 14th-century female Christian mystic Julian of Norwich is insistent that

> ...the revelations which she was given and the insights that followed from them were not for her own benefit alone...but where given for...all the ordinary mean and women of her time... she wrote in English, not French or Latin, so that her book could be read not just by the aristocracy or the clerical establishment by anyone able to read English; it could also be understood by anyone who had it read aloud to them. It was not restricted therefore to those--mostly clerics, therefore mostly men--who were well educated....She writes not only for those with special religious commitments but for everyone. Neither is her book full of demands and

imprecations. It is gentle, reassuring, even while it fosters ever-deepening trust in God.[212]

On the opposite side of the coin, you also find examples of spiritualities that do not work to be accessible and inclusive. A classic example here would be Freemasonry and other "secret" schools in the Western esoteric and gnostic traditions. Freemasonry, which is only one in a long line of exclusionary, esoteric, even feudal, spiritualities, although it purports to offer an authentic spiritual methodology of connection, nevertheless is a secretive invite-only organization with an emphasis on recruiting up and coming business people. Similarly, Scientology, despite its ostensible concern with global healing, free thought, and personal clearing/empowerment, is not an accessible or inclusive religion at all. It is a highly secretive organization that requires its "thetans" to pay hundreds of thousands of dollars for access to exclusive spiritual training.[213]

2. Grounded and Embodied

In addition to being accessible and inclusive, an authentic spirituality should also be grounded and embodied. Grounded and embodied means that an authentic spirituality will recognize the significance of

---

[212] Grace M. Jantzen, "Mysticism and Experience," *Religious Studies* 25, no. 3 (1989): xxi.

[213] Nededog, "How Scientology Costs Members up to Millions of Dollars, According to Leah Remini's Show."

the physical universe *and* the importance of the physical body (whether that body is human or otherwise) and will honour them as such. Rather than dismissing physical creation as some kind of degraded divine afterthought, as something we have to escape or graduate out of, or as something that must be tamed and restrained for human purposes, authentic spirituality recognizes and embraces the significance, power, and glory of physical creation.

We can state the issue quite plainly; physical creation is the vehicle of spirit, the temple of the Holy Spirit, the body of Consciousness, and the vessel of God. An authentic spirituality will always understand that the physical universe and the physical body are central features of spiritual creation and key sites for the movement of Spirit. Authentic spirituality and authentic practitioners will always embrace manifestation and incarnation with positive regard. Authentic spirituality will always treasure and respect life, the universe, and everything. If we may be so bold as to say, authentic spirituality always honours the body as an important and sacred vehicle for highest Self and highest Consciousness.

There are a few important implications of this grounded and embodied view of the physical universe and the physical body that we need to pay attention to. **First of all,** because an authentic spirituality is grounded in a healthy respect and awareness of the significance of the body as a vehicle for Consciousness, authentic spirituality always looks to the health, well-being, and improvement of the body and mind (i.e., the physical unit) as a fundamental goal. The body cannot operate at peak performance as a vehicle for consciousness if it is not mentally and psychologically healthy and whole. Therefore, authentic spirituality always looks to the improvement of physical existence. This means that you will not find an authentic spirituality condoning the degradation, damage, or destruction of the body or the world in any way. An authentic spirituality will condemn violence of all kinds, suffering, poverty, and the pollution of the physical (and psychic) environments as sacrileges against the body. An authentic spirituality will encourage and work toward manifesting salutatory and respectful conditions that preserve the natural world and that provide a nurturing environment for said body. Authentic spirituality teaches us to nurture the development and maintain the integrity of all physical creation, including the human body. It can be no other way. Physical creation is the site of the incarnation and manifestation of Spirit and we must respect, nurture, and protect this site above all other things. To do other than respect the body would make about as much sense as getting up in the morning and beating your car (or bike) with a sledgehammer before you drive it. That is stupid. The body is a vehicle for Consciousness and must always be respected as such.

The second implication of this standard of grounded and embodied spirituality has to do with our collective view of childhood, and the way we train and socialize our children. Obviously, if the physical body functions as a vehicle for Consciousness, then having a healthy body, having a healthy physical unit, is a base requirement for full expression of Consciousness and strong connection. In this context, protection and proper development of the physical unit through infancy, childhood, adolescence, and early adulthood are of critical importance. A damaged vehicle will be subject to mental and physical illness and will have problems awakening, activating, and connecting.

If the care and development of the body are critical, then when it comes to the proper development of the physical unit, our current parental and socialization practices are inadequate, because our current practices are quite toxic and damaging. I briefly outline the research that supports this statement in an article entitled "Toxic Socialization,"[214] where I also point out that "when definitions of abuse are liberal, just about everybody on the planet becomes a victim of abuse at some point, a fact which most can anecdotally confirm simply by examining their family, school, and work life. This is not a revelation that should be taken lightly since even single instances of emotional violence perpetrated

---

[214] Mike Sosteric, "Toxic Socialization," *Socjourn*, 2016, https://www.academia.edu/25275338/Toxic_Socialization.

by trusted adult figures can have long term debilitating consequences.[215]

Of course, upon reading this, some people mind find themselves struggling with **disjuncture.** Some might even find themselves justifying forms of violence and abuse in childhood as part of a necessary disciplinary process. Others may be ignoring their own habits and actions and tell themselves that they do a good job of raising their children to their full potential despite the fact that they are violent and abusive. Given the amount of research that demonstrates the debilitating impact of toxic socialization, and the rarity of the fully actualized and connected human being, these justifications are hard to sustain. If our socialization practices were better, if our spiritualities were more authentic, if we were better parents, if we treated people better, if we did a better job looking after each other, there wouldn't be so many angry and disconnected people raging about on this world.

Please understand, this should not be read as a judgmental slam against parenting or humanity in general, but merely as an appeal for self-honesty and a strong admonishment to change. We do not engage in toxic parental practices and we do not damage the physical body because we are evil or bad parents, but

---

[215] E.-M. Annerbäck et al., "Child Physical Abuse and Concurrence of Other Types of Child Abuse in Sweden—Associations with Health and Risk Behaviors," *Child Abuse & Neglect* 36 (July 1, 2012): 585–95.

because this is how our parents, priests, and professionals taught us to be; consequently, we believe we are doing the right thing. But, we are not. Toxic socialization damages the body and undermines our ability to connect. If we want to stop toxic socialization and develop socialization practices that do not damage and undermine the physical unit's ability to connect, our first step must be facing the truth and uncomfortable implications of our own actions. Once we do that, then it only requires a little support to actually change. And change we must. If we want to save the world, we cannot continue to turn out angry, diminished, and disconnected human beings. Toxic socialization practices must end immediately

Finally, **a third implication** of the embodied and grounded nature of authentic spirituality is that money is a key factor in the authentic spiritual unfolding of this planet, and therefore money should, as explained in *Rocket Scientists' Guide to Money and the Economy*,[216] be understood for what it really is, respected as an important tool of modern life, and distributed fairly and without exploitation. In an age where everything from clothing to food to housing costs, you simply cannot properly look after your physical unit without money. Nor, it should be noted, can you put aside the necessary

---

[216] Mike Sosteric, *Rocket Scientists' Guide to Money and the Economy: Accumulation and Debt.* (St Albert, Alberta: Lightning Path Press., 2016).

time for connection practice if you are working three jobs just to get by. If you cannot look after your physical unit, and if you are too busy simply trying to survive, you will have a hard time with authentic spiritual practice

Of course, to say that money is important and we all have to have enough doesn't mean we should pursue wealth accumulation beyond a need for satisfactory human comfort and protection. The callous accumulation of billions or the ostentatious purchase and display of Ninety-six Rolls Royce vehicles demonstrates not spiritual mastery, but egoism and addiction,[217] despite what many apologists might say. Money needs to be distributed fairly and distributed properly so everybody can heal and connect, just as it says in the Bible's new testament, in particular Acts 4: 32-37, where it shows early Christians redistributing their income so everyone can be taken care of, but, it also needs to be treated as the dangerous and addictive substance that it is; otherwise, the addiction will continue to destroy the world. [218]

---

[217] Mike Sosteric and Gina Ratkovic, *Lightning Path Workbook Two - Healing*, vol. 2, Lightning Path Workbook Series (St. Albert, Alberta: Lightning Path Press, 2017), https://press.lightningpath.org/product/the-lightning-path-book-two-healing/.

[218] Mike Sosteric, "How Money Is Destroying the World," *The Conversation*, 2018, https://theconversation.com/how-money-is-destroying-the-world-96517.

To summarize, the second pillar of authentic spirituality is all about grounded and embodied spirituality. In practice, this means that authentic spirituality will love and respect the natural world and the physical body, will hold childhood up as a critical and sacred time, and will take money seriously, knowing that everybody needs enough to survive and thrive. If you find any of these things absent on the path you are following, you are missing the second pillar, cannot build an authentic spirituality, and are probably following an inauthentic path.

As for the validity of this pillar, you do find a concern with grounded and embodied spirituality, including a concern for money and its proper distribution, in this world's authentic spiritual traditions. It it blatant in the Bible where it is written of earl Christians that.

> All the believers were one in heart and mind. No one claimed that any of their possessions was their own, but they shared everything they had... And God's grace was so powerfully at work in them all that there were no needy persons among them. For from time to time those who owned land or houses sold them, brought the money from the sales and put it at the apostles' feet, and it was distributed to anyone who had need (Acts 4: 32-37).

You also this grounded and embodied spirituality it in the concern for right environment of mystics like St. Teresa of Avila who, in her teachings, emphasizes the need for calm, safe, drama free environments.[219] You also find it in the almost ubiquitous concern to heal human illness and end human suffering characteristic of Christ's teachings, Buddha's teachings, and even other more modern traditions, like the dated and now largely defunct Arica School, started by Oscar Ichazo,[220] which places heavy emphasis on transcending a dysfunctional and bodily ego to achieve healthy reconnection.[221] You also find it in Zen Buddhism in an emphasis on empirical reality and cause and effect. For example, the Zen fable "Wild Fox Koan,"[222] teaches a very clear lesson about the importance of staying grounded to empirical realities. In

[219] St. Teresa of Avila, *The Way of Perfection*.

[220] Sam Keen, "Breaking the Tyranny of the Ego," in *Interviews with Oscar Ichazo* (New York: Arica Institute Press, 1982), 3-28, https://amzn.to/2MOwleU.

[221] I feel compelled to note here that while there is apparently value in Ichazo's connection framework, publications of the Aria school can be extremely expensive, and the vast majority of their "teachings" are only accessible to students behind an expensive pay wall. Although Ichazo's original desire was to have his school open and accessible to the world (apparently, Ariza means "open door"), even going so far as to say the school should be accessible to the working classes, the institute as currently instantiated fails on pillar one and pillar two. You can browse the Arica school at https://www.arica.org/

[222] A version is provided by Wikipedia at the following url: https://en.wikipedia.org/wiki/Wild_fox_koan. The irony of using a supernatural fable to teach the importance of cause and effect should not lost here.

this story, a Zen Master is turned into a fox to teach him a lesson about the importance of cause and effect and the wisdom of not pretending to be above it.[223]

3. Responsible and Non-Judgmental

Accessible and inclusive, grounded and embodied, are the first two pillars of authentic spirituality. The third pillar of authentic spirituality is the pillar of responsibility. To be as clear as possible, an authentic spirituality teaches broad responsibility, for your body, your family, your children, this society, and the entire world. Authentic spirituality neither teaches, encourages, expects, or requires you to turn away from reality, disrespect your own health, neglect your own children,[224] or ignore the suffering of this world. Authentic spirituality never teaches you to justify and accept anything that is unacceptable (like poverty) just so you can "attract" yourself some wealth. Authentic spirituality requires responsibility for all life on this planet, on a truly global scale. If a spirituality does not teach broad and general responsibility, then it is not authentic at all.

---

[223]Mike Sosteric, "The Wild Fox Koan," 2019, https://www.lightningpath.org/readings/the-wild-fox-koan/.

[224]Among other things, a remarkable story of neglect by the niece of Scientology ruler, David Miscavige: Miscavige Hill, "Beyond Belief: My Secret Life Inside Scientology and My Harrowing Escape EBook: Jenna Miscavige Hill, Lisa Pulitzer: Kindle Store."

The stipulation that authentic spiritualties should be responsible is an extension of the outcome measure, activation. As we've seen, activation is a consequence of authentic spirituality. One of the consequences of this activation is that people who have one or more connection experiences often become more active at home, at work, politically, and so on. Individuals following an authentic spirituality of connection realize things (they awaken), they take responsibility for things, and they take action. This is quite clear when we consider biographies of great spiritual leaders like Christ or Gandhi, or the activities of more modern teachers. Jesus Christ did not sit home and beam positive and loving thoughts into the cosmos, he got out and incited rebellion.[225] Similarly, Gandhi did not sit home drinking chai tea: he spent his entire life on the road, in South Africa and in his native India, fighting for Indian independence and justice or all people.[226]

The stipulation that an authentic spirituality should teach a responsibility founded on action is violated by many "New Age" spiritualties, which often encourage an

---

[225] E. Dyck, "'Hitting Highs at Rock Bottom': LSD Treatment for Alcoholism, 1950-1970," *Social History of Medicine* 19, no. 2 (August 2006): 313–29, https://doi.org/10.1093/shm/hkl039; Sosteric, "Rethinking the Origins and Purpose of Religion: Jesus, Constantine, and the Containment of Global Revolution."

[226] Gandhi, *Gandhi: An Autobiography*; Fisher, *The Life of Mahatma Gandhi*; Anonymous, "Gandhi and the Passive Resistance Campaign 1907-1914."

individual to abdicate responsibility and engage in passive non-action. Such is the case with so-called Law of Attraction (LOA) style spirituality. LOA pundits teach not action and responsibility, but avoidance and the abdication of responsible action in the world. They teach, for example, that to deal with war you don't go to anti-war rallies, you sit at home and send "positive intent... into the thought-substance of the mass consciousness."[227] They teach inaction and denial of responsibility in the face of reality. The denial of responsibility is quite explicit. As Law of Attraction (LOA) founder Esther Hicks said, "You did not come into this environment to create through action."[228] You come into this world to passively attract. All you have to do to get your big California mansion is "attract" it and voila. If you remain positive, it will happen.

Obviously, clearly, unequivocally, this is load of spiritual horseshit. Just like bridges require a lot of work from engineers, teachers, workers, etc. California mansions do not materialize without a lot of very hard work from a lot of hard-working people.

It is relatively easy to make a case that authentic spirituality should be responsible and should encourage

---

[227] Kenneth MacLean, "The Law of Attraction and War," EzineArticles, accessed June 3, 2019, https://ezinearticles.com/?The-Law-of-Attraction-and-War&id=280965.

[228] Neil Farber, "The Truth About the Law of Attraction," Psychology Today, accessed June 3, 2019, https://www.psychologytoday.com/blog/the-blame-game/201609/the-truth-about-the-law-attraction.

action in the world, since responsible, change-oriented action is a feature of many traditional and even modern (LOA aside), connection frameworks, as we saw earlier in the section on spiritual activation. But, what about the second part of this pillar, that authentic spirituality should be non-judgmental. How does that fit in?

To understand the relevance of teaching non-judgment, you have to understand two things. Number one, you have to understand something about guilt and shame. Guilt and shame are honest and natural human reactions to actions we know to be wrong. When experienced properly, guilt and shame are useful "self-adjustment" tools. The problem is, these emotions can be quite painful. When we do something we know is wrong and we experience these painful emotions, we have two choices. We can either acknowledge the source of the guilt and shame and change our behaviour, that is, we can take action in the world to make it more aligned with what we know to be correct, or, we can repress the truth of our actions and instead pretend that our actions are aligned and positive, even when they are not. Unfortunately, since change can be difficult, and since guilt and shame can be quite excruciating, even debilitating, there is psychological incentive to repress awareness and engage in avoidance.[229] More to the point,

---

[229] Darlene Lancer, JD, and MFT Last updated: 8 Oct 2018~ 3 min read, "Shame: The Core of Addiction and Codependency," Psych Central, May 17, 2016, https://psychcentral.com/lib/shame-the-core-of-addiction-and-codependency/; Cikanavicius, "Toxic, Chronic Shame."

our body's have a natural aversion to it. Our body's naturally seek to avoid the experience of pain, physical or emotional. When we experience pain, we look around for ways to reduce it. When it comes to guilt and shame, the natural response is to repress, avoid, and deny. We repress the actions that cause us guilt. We avoid taking responsibility. We deny that it ever happened.

This psychological incentive to repress brings us to the second reason why authentic spirituality should eschew judgment, guilt, and shame. Judgmental spiritualties encourage, even inflame, our sense of guilt and shame, thereby contributing, in a very direct way, to avoidance of toxic psychological repression and the avoidance of responsibility. You don't have to be Sigmund Freud to see that this avoidance happens all the time. Watch the people around you as they pathologically avoid experiencing guilt and shame by denying their actions and finding ways to blame others. Or, better yet, reflect upon your own actions and avoidance. The experience of guilt and shame leads to avoidance, and this avoidance leads directly to abdication of responsibility and action, and probably all sorts of emotional and psychological dysfunction.[230] Thus, a spirituality that is ostensibly about responsibility eschews the use of judgment because judgment

---

[230] The uber rich are particularly good at this. See the most excellent book by Anand Giridharadas, *Winners Take All: The Elite Charade of Changing the World* (New York: Knopf, 2018), https://amzn.to/2FDfF49.

enhances guilt and shame, and enhancing guilt and shame leads to avoidance of responsibility.

To summarize, the tendency to self-repression in response to guilt and shame is exacerbated by systems of inauthentic spirituality, psychology, and human development that are judgmental. When we feel judged, our guilt and shame are amplified. When our guilt and shame are amplified, self-repression and avoidance become much more likely. Obviously, a spirituality that claims to be authentic cannot be encouraging denial, self-repression, and avoidance. If a spirituality or religion utilizes guilt and shame to control behaviour, by definition, it cannot be authentic.

Is responsibility, as well as guilt and shame, a thing in various connection frameworks? It is. Most connection frameworks recognize the importance of responsibility, and even very corrupted ones will teach broad responsibility for others and the planet. The question, of course, is whether or not the framework's pundits "walk the talk." Many spiritualties teach broad responsibility, but then when you dip into their murky waters, you find their founders or their representative priests and gurus stashing the cash while the people around them suffer and starve. Obviously, a spirituality that does not practice what it preaches is not an authentic spirituality. A spirituality that does not teach responsibility, or a spirituality that presents as a hypocrisy, is not an authentic spirituality, period.

As for guilt, shame, and the avoidance of judgment, once again, this is a feature of authentic connection frameworks, especially those of the Western variety. Jesus Christ advised those seeking connection to forgive, let go, and "turn the other cheek." Other authentic world teachers do the same,[231] thereby pushing us to move beyond judgment and the toxicity that arises from the guilt that judgment induces, though sometimes there are profound contradictions. Curiously, most religions that arise from these teachings do not explicitly warn of the debilitating consequences of psychological and emotional guilt and shame; they exploit it to control their followers. This is true of very religions like Western Catholicism, which weaponizes guilt and shame to control its followers, and also the small and medium cult-like expressions you find popping out now and again. If a spirituality utilizes guilt and shame to control its base of followers, it is not an authentic spirituality.

4. Empowering

So far in our discussion of the pillars of authentic spirituality we have suggested that an authentic spirituality should be accessible and inclusive, grounded and embodied, and responsible and non-judgmental.

---

[231]Tom Netherland, "Doctrine of Forgiveness Vital to Most World Religions," HeraldCourier.com, accessed August 26, 2019, https://www.heraldcourier.com/lifestyles/doctrine-of-forgiveness-vital-to-most-world-religions/article_b3157727-7aec-5a67-9498-6fc3eac4c188.html.

The fourth pillar of authentic spirituality that should be present is empowerment.

Empowerment here is an extension of the outcome measure of activation noted in part two of this book. There, we noted that political, social, even familial activation is an outcome measure of authentic spirituality. Activation occurs when one awakens and becomes empowered to change situations for the better. When people make a connection, they awaken and are empowered to make changes and improve.

Since activation is an outcome measure of authentic spirituality, an authentic spirituality should recognize this activation by supporting and teaching empowerment, both at a personal level and a collective level. Authentic spiritualties should broadly teach we have authority over our own lives, and that we all have the authority to create, as we see fit. An authentic spirituality will teach that we are responsible, powerful, and sovereign and that we know the difference between what is right and wrong. As beings of independence and power, if we want something, we do not have to beg God, the fates, or anybody else. We just need to work for it. That is all.

Since authentic spiritualties teach empowerment, authentic spirituality must never be about "following the leader" or giving in to some external power. Authentic spirituality should not teach or train an individual to bow before authority, follow orders, believe in fate, or submit to outside and external powers, like God, "galactic rays," karma, or whatever. There is nothing wrong with guidelines, morality, rules, and expectations, but this should be coupled with teachings that empower and give people the authority to exist and create in the world, as they so choose, so long as we are uplifting and not harming others.

Because authentic spirituality is empowering, authentic spirituality should model empowerment and the devolution of authority. Authentic spirituality never supports and/or enacts the empowerment of the few over the disempowerment of the many, nor disguises the empowerment beneath the veneer of race or gender. If spirituality is to be authentic, it must reflect our fundamental equality and our true power and responsibility. It must never engage us in systems of hierarchy or authority intended to restrict, disempower, or exploit others, nor must it propagate ideologies that enslave, disempower, or teach submission to authority, whether that authority is "in heaven" or on an earthly throne. As noted by Starhawk, an authentic spirituality will eschew terms like High Priest and High Priestess and instead choose to work nonhierarchically.[232] Any

---

[232]Starhawk, *Spiral Dance, The - 20th Anniversary: A Rebirth of the Ancient Religion of the Goddess: 20th Anniversary Edition: Starhawk: 9780676974676: Gateway - Amazon.Ca* (New York: Harper One, 2011), https://www.amazon.ca/Spiral-Dance-Anniversary-Rebirth-Religion/dp/0062516329/ref=sr_1_1?keywords=the+spiral+dance&qid=1555076627&s=gateway&sr=8-1.

spirituality that acts and enacts hierarchy and disempowerment is not an authentic spirituality.

A case in point here is the exoteric Christian Church. The exoteric Church generally teaches the opposite of empowerment. They characterize their followers as sheeple and advise the sheep to listen to the rules and follow the good Sheppard, Christ. Notably, this is exactly the opposite of what Jesus taught, which was to stand up against exploitation and empire, and to work against poverty and suffering,[233] to "let your light shine" and do good works (Mathew 5: 15).

An authentic spirituality that honours empowerment should also emphasize peace and non-violence. Violence is *always* an attempt to disempower another individual through force. Violence is thus anathema in an authentic spirituality, because it means the denial of empowerment to others.

Violence itself can come in many forms, physical, emotional, and psychological, and an authentic spirituality will eschew all these forms. In general, any physical, verbal, or non-verbal act that is experienced as a threat or that actually hurts you in a physical, emotional, psychological, or spiritual way, is a violent act.

Most connection frameworks will give lip service to non-violence; however, not all traditions encourage their

---

[233]Sosteric, "Rethinking the Origins and Purpose of Religion: Jesus, Constantine, and the Containment of Global Revolution."

leaders and practitioners to practice what they preach, and some traditions actually encourage violence against others, so long as the "other" is evil. This is the case with the Western traditions based on Zoroastrian nodes introduced earlier. As noted earlier, these archetypal nodes encourage violence again those they define as "evil." In western traditions, the evil ones are to be violently destroyed and cast into the pits of hell.

It is not just western traditions that can be violent towards others. You will also find that some traditions encourage violence against those who are not within the tradition. The fascinating story of Bhagwan Shree Rajneesh (a.k.a. Osho), recounted in the Netflix documentary *Wild Wild Country*,[234] is a case in point. Members of this cult-ashram were emotionally and psychologically violent towards the local townspeople. They tried to rig local elections and they tried to poison the local people. They even developed a paramilitary "peace force"[235] which purchased numerous weapons to be used, ostensibly for defence. The arming began in January 18, 1983 when the ashram ordered a revolver, and continues forward from there.

---

[234]Way and Way, *Wild Wild Country*.

[235]The Oregonian, "Rajneeshees Establish Security Forces, Large Armory (Part 10 of 20)," oregonlive.com, July 10, 1985, https://www.oregonlive.com/rajneesh/1985/07/rajneeshees_establish_security.html.

> In two years' time, the inventory included at least 14 .357 Magnums; several other handguns; three riot guns; a Ruger Model 77 bolt-action, high-powered rifle with telescope sight; nine military-style semiautomatic weapons; and four tear gas grenades.
>
> The Rajneeshees discussed buying fully automatic weapons as early as 1982 [and] ...Within two years, however, the Rajneeshees saw a need for automatic weapons, making at least three attempts to buy them.

In addition to encouraging violence against "evil" others, you will also find that some traditions rely on violence, or the threat of this violence, to control their members and force compliance. My own childhood experience in the Catholic Church attests to this. The Catholic Church encourages actual physical violence against children (spare the rod and spoil the child) and also the threat of violence, the worst of which is the threat of eternal damnation for not following the rules, to control its passive membership. And of course, there are many traditions and cults where various forms of violence among members is a regular and daily occurrence.[236] If you have ever been a part of such a

---

[236]Miscavige Hill, "Beyond Belief: My Secret Life Inside Scientology and My Harrowing Escape EBook: Jenna Miscavige Hill, Lisa Pulitzer:

tradition or cult, or if you are a member of such a tradition now, a few moments of thought will suffice to reveal the violence to you.

To be clear, a connection framework that allows or encourages violence of any form is not an authentic tradition. It is basic psychology, really. Violence and assault cause physical, emotional, and mental distress. Violence and assault, even the threat of assault, damages the physical body and causes all sorts of psychological, emotional, and physical illness. Violence and the trauma that ensues from that violence damages the physical body.[237] More to the point, violence and assault *disconnects* the body from its own higher consciousness. Any tradition that operates with violence operates in the opposite direction of health and connection.

There are many examples of traditions that teach passivity and compliance, or that say they are about empowerment, but practice and implement the opposite. What's more important than enumerating all the traditions and schools which use violence against others or their own followers is to simply learn to identify them *in situ*, and avoid them when you do. If you are in a tradition where violence is involved, perhaps reconsider your membership. It is much better to recognize this inauthenticity early, not only because

---

Kindle Store"; Kohl, *Jonestown Survivor*.

[237] Once again, for an overview of the impact of violence and stress on the physical unit, see Sosteric, "Toxic Socialization."

violence (even emotional and psychological violence) does real damage and you want to stop that as soon as you can, but also because, as members of violent traditions will tell you, it can be difficult to extricate oneself once one has become embedded. Thankfully, red flags here are easy to spot. Hierarchy in a spiritual tradition is one red flag, as is the presence of various forms of violence. If hierarchy and violence are present in any way, shape, or form, your best bet is to avoid and get out.

5. Fruitful

At this point in our discussion, we have covered four of the seven pillars of authentic spirituality. The fifth pillar of authentic spirituality is fruitfulness, by which we mean simply that authentic spirituality should make a real and positive difference in your life, and the life of those you surround yourself with.

The notion that authentic spirituality should be fruitful relates directly back to the pillar of empowerment, and our earlier discussion of outcome measures. The notion that spirituality should be fruitful is, in fact, a restatement and extension of the requirement that authentic spirituality should lead to measurable and meaningful outcomes, and that it should be empowering. If you think back to the outcome measures we discussed earlier, a fruitful spirituality is one that leads to the outcomes of healing and connection. Healing leads to physical, emotional, psychological, and spiritual well being. Connection leads to awakening, activation, and ascension. The whole process is comprised of numerous "fruitful outcomes," including psychological breakthroughs,[238] emotional cleansing (i.e., the sudden dissipation of anger and envy),[239] improved self-esteem,[240] enhanced intellectual power,[241] reduction of existential angst, an increase in meaning and happiness,[242] self actualization,[243] a general increase of life satisfaction,[244] and even experience of transcendence and "cosmic consciousness."[245]

---

[238]Rahtz et al., "Transformational Changes in Health Status: A Qualitative Exploration of Healing Moments."

[239]R.M. Offord, *Jerry McAuley: An Apostle to the Lost* (New York: Forgotten Books, 2012), https://amzn.to/2UFacCr.

[240]Parish, *Create Your Personal Sacred Text: Develop and Celebrate Your Spiritual Life*.

[241]Hanes, "Unusual Phenomena Associated With a Transcendent Human Experience: A Case Study."

[242]*This Is It and Other Essays on Zen and Spiritual Experience*, Kindle Edition (Random House, 1973), https://amzn.to/2IYr2rv.

[243]Abraham Maslow and Clark E. Moustakas, "Self-Actualization People: A Study of Psychological Health," in *The Self: Explorations in Personal Growth* (Harper Colophon, 1956), 160–94.

[244]Ervin Laszlo, Stanislav Grof, and Peter Russell, *The Consciousness Revolution* (Las Vegas: Elf Rock Productions, 1999), 67, https://amzn.to/2TlOCmC.

[245]Edward Carpenter, *The Art of Creation: Essays on the Self and Its Powers* (Kindle Edition: Amazon, 1921), https://amzn.to/2OSE3lu.

One particularly interesting fruit of authentic spirituality practice worth isolation and investigation is freedom from all forms of addiction. Everybody is familiar with addiction to alcohol and drugs. But addictions in society are far more pervasive than that. We can be addicted to substances, like drugs and alcohol, but also to high carbohydrate and high fat processed foods, to shopping, to exercise, to sex, and even to money.[246] You know you are addicted when you get to point where you spend all your time seeking out and interacting with that addiction, and no time on other important things, like family, friends., spiritual practice, and so on.

Because of the toxic condition of the world we live in, addiction is a pervasive problem. Most people end up addicted to something. Most people turn to something to ease the pain of samsara (the physical world), or to give them feelings of euphoria and pleasure which are absent from their daily life.

For your information, addiction is actually a common problem identified in the spiritual literature of this planet, especially Buddhism and Vedanta where it is discussed as *desire* or *attachment* to worldly things. The *Crest Jewel of Wisdom* by Shankara,[247] for example, spends a lot of time talking about addiction to money, power, ego aggrandizement, and so on. The text says that

---

[246]Sosteric, "How Money Is Destroying the World."

[247]Adi Sankaracharya, *The Crest-Jewel of Wisdom* (St. Albert, 2019).

desire/addiction undermines your spiritual progress by attaching you to the dramas and baubles of the material world, thereby distracting you from connection and connection practice. As a consequence of your addictions, you become locked in normal consciousness and stuck in the delusional world of samsara, which is true, and makes perfect sense. If you spend all your body's energy on denying your addictions and trying to find your next fix, for example, if you work all the time to "make money" or you get caught up in all the vamporous dramas of a disconnected world, you don't have any energy left for self-reflection, self-analysis, and connection practice. If you don't have any energy left, you won't make any spiritual progress forward.

What is the solution to addiction? Authentic spirituality! In the *Crest jewel*, we learn that authentic spiritual practice frees you from addiction/attachment. This freedom can occur gradually and over time, as we slowly begin to realize the nature of the addiction and its negative impact on our lives, but it can occur instantly, as the biography of Bill Wilson attests, as the consequence of a powerful connection experience.[248]

The relationship between addiction and authentic spirituality is something to consider when evaluating a spirituality or religion for its authenticity. If the spirituality is authentic, it should not only address

---

[248] Alcoholics Anonymous, *'PASS IT ON' The Story of Bill Wilson and How the A.A. Message Reached the World*.

addiction, as The *Crest Jewel* does, but it should also be successful in treating a person's addictions; or rather, the person following an authentic spirituality should find success in treating their own addictions. Whether the fruitful cure is experienced instantly as the miraculous outcome of a connection event, or over time in a process of growing awareness and personal change, one of the fruitful outcomes of authentic spirituality practice is the reduction and eventual elimination of addiction in its practitioners. If you're not seeing or experiencing this fruitful outcome, that's a seven pillars, alarm-raising red flag.

As a final comment, it may be useful to reiterate what we said earlier, which is that authentic spirituality should teach and emphasize the significance and importance of fruitful outcomes in the present. That is, spiritualties should not suggest that your primary benefit from spiritual practices comes in the next life, through entrance into "heaven," the avoidance of rebirth, the enjoyment of celestial "virgins," or whatever. Authentic spiritualties assert the benefits of practice in the here and now. If a religion or spirituality is avoiding the discussion of fruitful outcomes in the here and now and instead of distracting you with fantasies of after-life salvation, look away.

6. Logical and Consistent

So far we have discussed five of the seven pillars of authentic spirituality which are that an authentic spirituality should be accessible and inclusive, grounded and embodied, responsible and non-judgmental, empowering and fruitful. In addition to all these, an authentic spirituality should also be logical and consistent. That is, authentic spirituality should never be irrational, inconsistent, or illogical. This bears repetition often. Authentic spirituality should always be logical, consistent, and make total sense.

For some, the notion that authentic spirituality should be logical and consistent might seem like spiritual antitheses, After all, when we speak of human spirituality, we are talking about an immaterial and invisible universe of Consciousness. In other words, God, or however you want to refer to it. This has always been a matter of faith, has it not? There is no concrete evidence that such a thing actually exists, some will say; thus, in the context of human spirituality, logic, consistency, and common sense are, by definition, impossible.

In fact, however, they are not. Authentic spirituality can and should be logical, grounded, and consistent, with its own assumptions and propositions and with everything fitting together in a sensible way. It should never step outside the bounds of reason and common sense. As soon as spirituality starts to become illogical, inconsistent, or too far out of touch with what we generally recognize as logical common sense, we have a problem. This is true whether or not you prefer to rely on "natural" explanations of connection (i.e. neurological explanations) or whether you openly consider transcendent and transpersonal explanations.

It is important to underline this point. Logic and common sense can apply to both naturalistic explanations of spiritual phenomenon *and* to any "supernatural" explanations that may be invoked to explain the observable phenomenon (like connection experiences and connection outcomes) that attend authentic spirituality.

It might sound outrageous, especially to the fundamentalist atheist, but it is true, and we are not the first to assert this. Oscar Ichazo, founder of the Arica school, makes logic, rationality, and a "scientifically systematized" spirituality a central goal of human endeavor.[249] You can even apply logic and common sense to supernatural phenomenon. In fact, some might say that logic, common sense, and the mounting evidence provided by the study of connection experiences demands not only that we consider non-materialist explanations for some of the things we experience, but

---

[249]Oscar Ichazo, *The Human Process of Enlightenment and Freedom* (New York: Arica Institute, 1976).

that we accept these explanations as the most logical and parsimonious available. As Shear[250] points out

> From a common-sense perspective, we are intimately aware of consciousness, and it is a truism that consciousness has a variety of properties (among them qualia, intentionality, and non-spatiality) that are so different from those of matter that it is difficult if not impossible to see how consciousness could ever have been produced by matter. The problems that arise here are formidable, and have given rise to what has recently become popularized as 'the hard problem' of explaining the existence of consciousness in a material universe.

The "hard problem" is the problem of what consciousness is exactly, and how it arises. It is often assumed by lay people (and many scientists) that scientists feel this is a done deal, that scientists all agree that consciousness arises in the physical body, in the neurology of the brain and CNS. Put another way, it is assumed that scientists all believe that when your brain dies, you die. In fact, this is not the case. Consciousness as a phenomenon, and connection experiences which intimate transcendent realities, have not been

---

[250]"Mysticism and Scientific Naturalism," *Sophia* 43, no. 1 (May 2004): 85, https://doi.org/10.1007/BF02782439.

satisfactorily explained in materialist terms. Some scientists,[251] myself included, do indeed propose transcendent realities as logical and necessary explanations for what has been scientifically observed. We can arbitrarily dismiss these issues and these conclusions if we want, and no doubt some readers are fighting hard the intellectual inclination to do so, but as one scholar politely noted,[252] "if a physicist or a cognitive scientist suggests that consciousness can be explained in physical terms, this is merely a hope ungrounded in current theory, and the question remains open."

The point here isn't to get into a debate about the origins of consciousness. The point here is to emphasize the need for logic and consistency. Whatever your particular feeling about the nature of consciousness and connection, whatever side of the fence you are on *vis a vis* the role of religion, connection experience, and consciousness in human existence, it all needs be logical and consistent. Our thinking has to be logical and consistent, and any ideas we have about connection, what it is, how to obtain it, and what's it all for, have to be logical and consistent as well.

It is possible and it is important, because without logic and consistently, you get cockamamie nuttiness.

---

[251] See for example Dossey, "Nonlocal Mind: A (Fairly) Brief History of the Term"; Laszlo, Grof, and Russell, *The Consciousness Revolution*; Dossey, *Recovering the Soul: A Scientific and Spiritual Search*.

[252] *The Conscious Mind: In Search of a Fundamental Theory*, Kindle (New York: Oxford University Press, 1996), https://amzn.to/2Vzq5HW.

Consider the following anecdotal example. A few years ago, I read an article that suggested the problem of obesity in America was in fact not a problem at all. According to one spiritual "pundit," obesity was a good thing because it was a sign of enlightenment! People who became enlightened often developed "Buddha belly," said this writer. The conclusion? Adipose tissue was a sign of closeness to God! Surprise surprise. The fact that more and more individuals in North America were experiencing the Buddha belly (otherwise known as the obesity epidemic) was not the result of processed food and an advertising industry working overtime to addict the population to fat and sugar, it was the result of spiritual maturity.

Obviously, this pundit's notion that enlightenment causes obesity was not logical, it was ignorant, uneducated, and absurd. Not only that, it was dangerous. They had no sense of the health problems that attend obesity (like heart disease, diabetes, joint failure, etc.), no sense of the dangers of junk/processed foods in the diet of North Americans, and no sense of the impact of the mass media and advertising on encouraging greater consumption of junk foods. To be sure, there are different body types. It is also true that heavyset individuals can be perfectly healthy, but that is not always the case. Obesity, especially when attended by inactivity and poor diet, can lead to various problems. It has nothing to do with enlightenment and everything to do with lifestyle.

The example of "Buddha Belly" may seem trivial; nevertheless, it illustrates a point—some people don't apply logic and common sense to their spirituality, and that is a problem. Our spirituality and our thinking about it should be logical and common sensible. Sadly, often, it is not.

When wagging the finger at illogic and insensibility, we would not want to blame the general population. The failure here is often a failure of scholarship, not mass thinking. It is the scholar's job to sort shit out, to examine the phenomenon, and to explain the world. When scholars assume that human spirituality is silliness, when they suggest that no "serious" scholar would ever take it seriously, as one of my colleagues recently did to me, when they dismiss it all as "savage supernaturalism" as sociological "luminary" Peter Berger embarrassingly did in his book *A Rumor of Angels*,[253] it is not the people's fault, it is the scholar's fault. When scholars reject the area outright, perhaps without ever really taking a serious look, they leave a vacuum where all sorts of flighty, frivolous, and even dangerous nonsense can squeak its way in. There are even dire political consequences for their (our) lack of involvement. Butler[254] argues that scholar's, in particular progressive scholars, disinclination to get involved in

---

[253]Peter Berger, *A Rumor of Angels* (New York: Anchor Books, 1970).

human spirituality has left a vacuum that has been hijacked by conservative political interests, with increasingly detrimental global effect, as evinced by the international rise of nationalist and right-wing politics.[255]

The point here is simple: logic and consistency should apply as a pillar of authenticity throughout the corpus, and scholarly involvement can help make that happen, if they get over their own intellectual prejudice. It is not without precedent. August Comte, founding father of sociology, wrote *The Catechism of Positivism; or, Summary Exposition of the Universal Religion*. In this book, Comte literally tries to start a new religion. In the book, he outlines what he thinks is a logical and rational alternative to the religious offerings of his day.[256] This book is not recommend for reading because it is dry, pedantic, boring, tiresome, sexist, and prejudiced, but it is worthwhile that sociologists and their students ar aware of it, since it provides precedent for an academic getting involved in and even trying to start a religion. Similarly, Star Hawk, a feminist psychologist, has contributed to the development of Wicca and Goddess

---

[254]*Born Again: The Christian Right Globalized* (New York: Pluto Press, 2006).

[255]Mike Sosteric, "How the Conservative Right Hijacks Religion," *The Conversation*, 2019, https://theconversation.com/how-the-conservative-right-hijacks-religion-109218.

[256]Auguste Comte, *The Catechism of Positivism; or, Summary Exposition of the Universal Religion* (London: John Chapman, 1852), https://amzn.to/2I7oSRY.

worship.[257] However, none of these succeeded in bringing a logical, grounded, sensible framework into the mainstream of scholarly attention or larger society. Comte's effort was spiritually unsophisticated, and even though Wiccan religions, druidic worship, shamanism, and other forms of paganism are proliferating,[258] they nevertheless stay on the margin, and often suffer the same insensibility and illogic of mainstream traditions. Take the example of druids, who presumably base their spirituality on ancient Roman and Celtic traditions. Richard Hutton points out that except for a couple of vague references in the historical record, druid-ship has no historical roots at all. In fact, druidship is an imaginative construction.[259] Druids make druidism out to be whatever they want it to be. Of course, there's nothing wrong with fantasy cosplay, as long as you don't take it as representative of authentic spirituality, and as long as you stay logical, grounded, and consistent. Obviously, when a group of people just make stuff up to suit their own fantasy predilections, this is neither

---

[257] Starhawk, *Spiral Dance, The - 20th Anniversary: A Rebirth of the Ancient Religion of the Goddess: 20th Anniversary Edition: Starhawk: 9780676974676: Gateway - Amazon.Ca*.

[258] Kathryn Rountree, "Transforming Deities: Modern Pagan Projects of Revival and Reinvention.," *International Journal for the Study of New Religions* 8, no. 2 (July 2017): 213–36; Rosemary Radford Ruether, "The Normalization of Goddess Religion," *Feminist Theology* 13, no. 2 (January 2005): 151–57.

[259] Ronald Hutton, *The Druids* (London: Hambledon Continuum, 2007).

logical nor consistent with existing spiritual knowledge, nor is it authentic in any way. It might be fun from a play perspective, but if one is seeking an authentic spiritual practice, it is a total waste of time.

7. Empirical and Verifiable

At this point in our discussion, we have covered six of the seven pillars of authentic spirituality. Authentic spirituality should be accessible and inclusive, grounded and embodied, responsible and non-judgmental, empowering, fruitful, and logical. The final pillar of authentic spirituality is empirical verifiability. This pillar represents the simple requirement that authentic spirituality should, within reason, be empirically grounded and verifiable. Put another way, there has to be something real going on. There has to be more to spirituality than just snake oil and empty words. There should be evidence that it heals and connects.

While some might doubt that you can put spirituality to the empirical test, at this point, this shouldn't be a controversial statement at all. The entire journey up to here has been an empirical journey of setting standards, examining outcome measures, and comparing and contrasting authentic versus inauthentic spiritualties, based on empirical evidence. By now, we should understand, human spirituality and the connection experiences which root it are real and verifiable things which you can fruitfully analyze and meaningfully investigate. As Shear notes, obvious:

> ...such experiences are, like any other experiences, obviously capable of being studied scientifically. Indeed, more than a thousand of studies of physiological, psychological and behavioral correlates and effects of such experiences and procedures designed to produce them have been published over the last thirty years [260]

Indeed, this is true. "Such experiences [are] obviously capable of being studied scientifically," and from a variety of angles. You can study it psychologically, creating survey's[261] and researching the contribution of the experience to mental health and well being,[262] as American psychologist Abraham Maslow did.[263] You can,

---

[260] Shear, "Mysticism and Scientific Naturalism," 83.

[261] Ralph W. Hood Jr et al., "Dimensions of the Mysticism Scale: Confirming the Three-Factor Structure in the United States and Iran," *Journal for the Scientific Study of Religion* 40, no. 4 (2001): 691–705.

[262] Kevin R. Byrd, Delbert Lear, and Stacy Schwenka, "Mysticism as a Predictor of Subjective Well-Being," *International Journal for the Psychology of Religion* 10, no. 4 (2000): 259–69.

[263] A. H. Maslow, "Lessons from the Peak-Experiences," Journal of Humanistic Psychology 2.1 (1962), A. H. Maslow, Religions, Values, and Peak Experiences (Columbus: Ohio State University Press, 1964), A. H. Maslow, Towards a Psychology of Being (2nd Edition) (New York: Van Nostrand Reinhold Company, 1968), A.H. Maslow, The Farther Reaches of Human Nature (New York: Viking, 1971).

study the history of the phenomenon throughout the Eastern[264] and Western[265] world, as Andrew Harvey and Arthur Versluis did. You can study the neurology of the phenomenon.[266] Despite the fact that sociologists have largely ignored the phenomenon, you can even study it sociologically. Indeed, there are many interesting sociological things to say about connection experience. You can research the social class correlates of connection experience.[267] You can examine how authentic spirituality and authentic connection events can lead to progressive political transformation.[268] You can look at how elites consciously and deliberately co-opt human spirituality and bend it to serve their own agenda.[269] You can even write narratives about how spiritual leaders like Jesus Christ were not reactionary conservatives bent on oppressing women and minorities

---

[264] Harvey, *Teachings of the Hindu Mystics*.

[265] Arthur Versluis, *The Secret History of Western Sexual Mysticism* (Rochester, Vermont: Destiny Books, 2008); Arthur Versluis, *Magic and Mysticism: An Introduction to Western Esotericism* (Maryland: Rowman and Littlefield, 2007).

[266] Sosteric, "The Science of Ascension: The Healing Power of Connection."

[267] Linda Brookover Bourque and Kurt W. Back, "Language, Society and Subjective Experience," *Sociometry* 34, no. 1 (1971): 1–21.

[268] Sosteric, "Mystical Experience and Global Revolution."

[269] Mike Sosteric, "A Sociology of Tarot," <u>Canadian Journal of Sociology</u> 39.3 (2014). Also see Sosteric, "From Zoroaster to Star Wars, Jesus to Marx: The Science and Technology of Mass Human Behaviour."

at all, but anti-status quo revolutionaries[270] devoted to overthrowing elite power structures.

As you can see, there is absolutely no reason to believe that the productive attention of science cannot be turned to an empirical examination of connection experience. To suggest otherwise is to betray one's intellectual prejudice and empirical naiveté *vis a vis* the phenomenon of connection experience. Really, at this point, there is nothing revolutionary on the table at all. To say we expect empirical verifiability is to simply state what a few scholars already know, and more scholars and people need to know. Not only can we talk about, theorize, and even have connection experiences in a logical and sensible way, we can study connection experience in a rigorous and empirical way as well. "Mysticism" needs to have no part in any of this.

As a final note, while we should approach human spirituality from an empirical perspective, this empirical perspective should not prevent theorization and speculation, nor should it be used to ridicule and suppress those who do theorize and speculate, even when this theorization and speculation is outside the boundaries of established canon. The story of Rupert Sheldrake, a Cambridge trained Oxford scientists who was literally excommunicated from science for daring to

---

[270] Phill Gasper, "Jesus the Revolutionary?," *Socialist Worker*, 2011, https://socialistworker.org/2011/12/14/jesus-the-revolutionary. Sosteric, Rock and Roll Jesus.

speculate about a non-material reality, is an embarrassment to scientists everywhere.[271] Keep in mind, gravity was postulated as an *invisible* force of nature by Newton in the 17th century, but gravity itself was never actually observed, and consequently remained only a theory, until September 14, 2015 when Einstein's prediction of gravity waves was finally directly observed,[272] bringing scientists one step closer, ironically, to what mystics have always known,[273] which is that the universe is a vast cosmic ocean of consciousness, and all things in it merely waves in that ocean.

But, we digress.

The point here is that science can research human spirituality and it can contribute not only to the empirical verifiability of human spirituality, but to its logic and consistency as well. If this is true, and there no reason to think that it is not, then there is no reason not to demand that if a human spirituality is to be considered authentic, it should be logical and consistent, as per pillar six, as well as verifiable and empirically grounded, as per pillar seven. If you are finding the absence of either, you are probably not facing an authentic spiritual path.

---

[271] A. Freeman, "The Sense of Being Glared At: What Is It LIke to Be a Heretic?," *Journal of Consciousness Studies* 12, no. 6 (2005): 4–9.

[272] https://en.wikipedia.org/wiki/First_observation_of_gravitational_waves.

[273] BOL

Summary

In this chapter, we have examined the seven pillars of authentic spirituality. As noted, authentic spirituality should be accessible and inclusive, grounded and embodied, responsible and non-judgmental, empowering, fruitful, logical and consistent, and empirically verifiable. These pillars are not optional. If a spirituality is authentic, these seven pillars must be present. What is more, aspiring to them is not enough. You cannot just say, "We accept these standards and we will try to do our best." Just like an engineer building bridges must be able to guarantee their adherence to standards, so also must an authentic spirituality guarantee adherence to these pillars before we can call it authentic. If even one of these pillars is missing, something is wrong, and the spirituality is not authentic.

As a final comment allow me to say that in my view it is important not to loosen standards or backtrack on these pillars. As we have seen, even mentally ill people can have authentic spiritual experiences. there are consequences to inauthentic spirituality. These consequences range from time wasted on inauthentic and impotent practices, to the horrific cyanide deaths of Jonestown.

> The deaths in Jonestown took anywhere between five and 20 minutes. First, your entire body starts to convulse. Then your

mouth fills with a mixture of saliva, blood and vomit. Then you pass out, and then you die. Your body is deprived of oxygen completely. It's a horrific death.[274]

Religion and human spirituality are no different than civil engineering and the building of bridges. In both cases, lives are stake. In both cases, standards are required. In both cases, unnecessary death results from the abdication of standards. Religion or engineering, in the end, there is simply no excuse for that.

---

[274] Adam Janos, "What Was It Like to Die of Cyanide Poisoning at Jonestown?," A&E, accessed June 24, 2019, https://www.aetv.com/real-crime/jonestown-how-did-it-feel-to-die-of-cyanide-poisoning.

Conclusion

This, finally, brings us to the end of this *Rocket Scientists' Guide to Authentic Spirituality*. In this book, we have examined *outcome measures* and the *seven pillars of authentic spirituality*. Both of these offerings are different ways to look at the problem of human spirituality, and both help us increase our spiritual standards and the sophistication with which we approach the topic.

So, what are you going to do with this information? In the end, of course, the path you follow is your choice. After reading this book, you have two choices. Choice number one is to continue in the direction you are already going in and hope that it takes you somewhere good. Keep your traditional atheism and go on ignoring human spirituality despite its obvious relevance to things. Keep your dogmatic and ungrounded spirituality and hope for the best. Choice number two is to do a full one hundred and eighty-degree turn, and plow full steam ahead in a new spiritual and scientific direction.

You can decide for yourself what you want to do but if you want my advice, when it comes to building real bridges across real chasms, or building a bridge/connection to your own highest Consciousness, do not sit on your proverbial buttocks and do not settle for anything less than total spiritual/scientific truth. This is not a game, after all, and real lives are at stake not only on a small cult scale, but on a global scale as well.

Scientists long ago sounded a planetary emergency and it is getting worse with each passing day. The planet, human life, and all life on Earth in fact, is in jeopardy. Your soul, if you believe in that, is above it all and goes on happily no matter happens to this Earth; your body and human society, however, do not. They are under very real threat.

And just what does this threat have to do with authentic spirituality? Decades ago, while the world was ramping up for WWII, Alert Einstein commented on the nature of religion and its importance to the evolution and survival of humanity. At that time, he made a distinction between the original and authentic teachings of human spirituality and the "subsequent additions," which he felt corrupted the original teachings. Einstein did not have a lot of respect for the "subsequent additions," but he did have a lot of respect for the spirituality he felt was buried in ancient teachings. He said that these traditional teachings could cure all our social ills and save humanity from destruction. His position on this is not equivocal.

> If one purges the Judaism of the Prophets and Christianity as Jesus Christ taught it of all **subsequent additions**, especially those of the priests, one is left with a teaching which

is capable of curing all the social ills of humanity.[275]

Although not using the nomenclature introduced in this book, Einstein is making a clear distinction between authentic and inauthentic spirituality, and he is making a clear statement on the value of the former. Einstein wasn't very clear on what made authentic spirituality authentic, and his thinking on connection experience was a little muddled, but he did intimate he had mild connection experiences himself,[276] and he did think these were valuable for personal, scientific, social, and political reasons. We absolutely agree. Authentic spirituality has important connection outcomes (i.e. healing, awakening, etc.) which are valuable for personal, scientific, social, and political reasons. As we have also seen, authentic spirituality does not have to be detached from common sense pillars and standards. We can think about and assert standards that not only help us evaluate current spiritual offerings, but also help us develop modern, sensible, embodied, logical, accessible, inclusive, empowering, fruitful, and rational scientific alternatives, which honour the foundations but provide a more sophisticated and more effective experience.

---

[275]Albert Einstein, *The World as I See It*, Kindle (Samaira Book Publishers, 2018), https://amzn.to/2NR8B6z: emphasis added.

[276]William Hermanns, *Einstein and the Poet* (Boston: Branden Books, 1983), https://amzn.to/2EXiooQ; Einstein, *The World as I See It*; Albert Einstein, *Out of My Later Years* (Citadel Press, 2000).

Seriously. Science has made significant, revolutionary even miraculous contributions in every area of human interest and concern *except* human spirituality. There is no reason to expect that it cannot do the same for human spirituality. All we have to do is get over our intellectual prejudice long enough to a) reject the tropes that suggest that spirituality and science are antithesis and b) take a closer look. Once we do take a closer, open-minded look we will see, there is something in human spirituality, something in connection experience, something ancient and long ignored by modern science, something incredible and of deep human significance, that, if as a species we want to survive, we simply cannot ignore any longer.

About the Author

Mike Sosteric is a sociologist with a specialization in psychology, religion, occult studies, "mysticism," and social inequality. After a series of dramatic connection events caused him to question the materialist foundation of modern science, he began practicing and exploring connection, from a sociological and psychological perspective.

References

Abad-Santos, Alex. "Lizard People: The Greatest Political Conspiracy Ever Created." Vox, November 5, 2014. https://www.vox.com/2014/11/5/7158371/lizard-people-conspiracy-theory-explainer.

Adam, James. *The Religious Teachers of Greece*. Gifford Lectures. New Jersey: Reference Book Publishers, 1965. https://www.giffordlectures.org/books/religious-teachers-greece.

Alcoholics Anonymous. *'PASS IT ON' The Story of Bill Wilson and How the A.A. Message Reached the World*. Kindle. New York: AA World Services, 1984. https://amzn.to/2XKQNP5.

Annerbäck, E.-M., L. Sahlqvist, C.G. Svedin, G. Wingren, and P.A. Gustafsson. "Child Physical Abuse and Concurrence of Other Types of Child Abuse in Sweden—Associations with Health and Risk Behaviors." *Child Abuse & Neglect* 36 (July 1, 2012): 585–95.

Anonymous. "Gandhi and the Passive Resistance Campaign 1907-1914." Text. South African History Online, July 30, 2013. https://www.sahistory.org.za/article/gandhi-and-passive-resistance-campaign-1907-1914.

Bakker, Arnold B. "Flow among Music Teachers and Their Students: The Crossover of Peak Experiences." *Journal of Vocational Behavior* 66, no. 1 (February 1, 2005): 26–44. https://doi.org/10.1016/j.jvb.2003.11.001.

Barkun, Michael. *A Culture of Conspiracy: Apocalyptic Visions in Contemporary America*. California: University of California Press, n.d.

Bartolome de las Casas. *A Brief Account of the Destruction of the Indies*. London: R. Hewson, 1552.

Bennett, Chris. *Liber 420: Cannabis, Magickal Herbs and the Occult*. Walterville, OR: Trine Day, 2018.

Berger, Peter. *A Rumor of Angels*. New York: Anchor Books, 1970.

Bernard Starr. "Why Christians Were Denied Access to Their Bible for 1,000 Years." *Huffpost Religion*, July 20, 2013.

Bidney, Martin. "Epiphany in Autobiography: The Quantum Changes of Dostoevsky and Tolstoy." *Journal of Clinical Psychology* 60, no. 5 (May 2004): 471–80.

Blazer, John A. "An Experimental Evaluation of 'Transcendence of Environment.'" *Journal of Humanistic Psychology* 3, no. 1 (1963): 49–53.

Booker, Christopher. *The Neophiliacs: Revolution in English Life in the Fifties and Sixties*. New York: Harper Collins, 1970.

Bourque, Linda Brookover, and Kurt W. Back. "Language, Society and Subjective Experience." *Sociometry* 34, no. 1 (1971): 1–21.

Boyce, Mary. *Zoroastrians: Their Religious Beliefs and Practices*. Routledge, 2001.

Bruneau, Marie-Florine. *Women Mystics Confront the Modern World*. Albany: State University of New York Press, 1998. https://amzn.to/2L1L0m2.

Bucke, R. M. *Cosmic Consciousness: A Study in the Evolution of the Human Mind*. Kindle Edition. California: The Book Tree, 2006. https://amzn.to/2IjxuaC.

Butler, Jennifer. *Born Again: The Christian Right Globalized*. New York: Pluto Press, 2006.

Byrd, Kevin R., Delbert Lear, and Stacy Schwenka. "Mysticism as a Predictor of Subjective Well-Being." *International Journal for the Psychology of Religion* 10, no. 4 (2000): 259–69.

Carhart-Harris, R. L., and K. J. Friston. "The Default-Mode, Ego-Functions and Free-Energy: A Neurobiological Account of Freudian Ideas." *Brain* 133, no. 4 (28 08/16/received 12/23/revised 12/23/accepted 2010): 1265–83. https://doi.org/10.1093/brain/awq010.

Carpenter, Edward. *The Art of Creation: Essays on the Self and Its Powers*. Kindle Edition: Amazon, 1921. https://amzn.to/2OSE3lu.

Castaneda, Carlos. *The Teachings of Don Juan: A Yaqui Way of Knowledge, 40th Anniversary Edition*. New York: Washington Square Press, 1996.

Caswell, Arthur. "The Code of Handsome Lake, The Seneca Prophet." *University of the State of New York Education Department Bulletin* 530 (1912). http://www.rickgrunder.com/parallels/mp305.pdf.

Chalmers, David. *The Conscious Mind: In Search of a Fundamental Theory*. Kindle. New York: Oxford University Press, 1996. https://amzn.to/2Vzq5HW.

Cikanavicius, Darius. "Toxic, Chronic Shame: What It's Like to Live with It." Psych Central.com, 2019. https://blogs.psychcentral.com/psychology-self/2019/01/toxic-chronic-shame/.

Clarke, Arthur C. *Childhood's End*. New York: Del Rey, 1987.

Climacus, John. *The Ladder of Divine Ascent*. Toronto: Patristic Publishing, 2017.

Comte, Auguste. *The Catechism of Positivism; or, Summary Exposition of the Universal Religion*. London: John Chapman, 1852. https://amzn.to/2I7oSRY.

Cortright, Brant. "An Integral Approach to Spiritual Emergency." *Guidance & Counseling* 15, no. 3 (2000): 12.

Davids, T. W. Rhys. *The Book of the Great Decease - The Maha-Parinibbana-Sutta*. Translated by Translated from Pali by T. W. Rhys Davids. Kindle Edition. Amazon Digital Services, n.d. https://amzn.to/2XKQpjC.

De Christopher, Dorothy. "I Am the Root of a New Tradition." In *Interviews with Oscar Ichazo*, 129–54. New York: Arica Institute Press, 1982. https://amzn.to/2MOwleU.

Dick, B. *The Oxford Group and Alcoholics Anonymous*. Kindle Edition. Kihei, Maui: Paradise Research Publications, 2011. https://amzn.to/2VPeVP3.

Dossey, Larry. "Nonlocal Mind: A (Fairly) Brief History of the Term." *Explore: The Journal of Science and Healing* 11, no. 2 (2015): 89–101. http://dx.doi.org/10.1016/j.explore.2014.12.001.

———. *Recovering the Soul: A Scientific and Spiritual Search*. Toronto: Bantam Books, 1989.

———. *Space, Time, and Medicine*. Vol. 11. Boston: Shambhala Publications, 1982. https://amzn.to/2Vs6nBL.

Dr. Charles A. Eastman. "Sioux Mythology." In *The International Folk-Lore Congress of the World's Columbian Exposition*, edited by Hellen Wheeler Basett and Frederick Starr, I:221–26. Charles H. Sergel Company, 1898.

Dyck, E. "'Hitting Highs at Rock Bottom': LSD Treatment for Alcoholism, 1950-1970." *Social History of Medicine* 19, no. 2 (August 2006): 313–29. https://doi.org/10.1093/shm/hkl039.

Ehrman, Bart D. *Misquoting Jesus: The Story Behind Who Changed the Bible and Why*. Harper One, 2007.

Einstein, Albert. *Out of My Later Years*. Citadel Press, 2000.

———. *The World as I See It*. Kindle. Samaira Book Publishers, 2018. https://amzn.to/2NR8B6z.

Elkins, David. "Why Humanistic Psychology Lost Its Power and Influence in American Psychology." *Journal of Humanistic Psychology* 49, no. 1 (2009): 267–91.

Ellens, J. Harold. *Seeking the Sacred with Psychoactive Substances: Chemical Paths to Spirituality and to God*. California: Praeger, 2014.

Ernst, Carl W. *Teachings of Sufism*. Boston: Shambhala, 1999.

Farber, Neil. "The Truth About the Law of Attraction." Psychology Today. Accessed June 3, 2019. https://www.psychologytoday.com/blog/the-blame-game/201609/the-truth-about-the-law-attraction.

Fisher, Louis. *The Life of Mahatma Gandhi*. New York: Harper & Row, 1950.

Fiske, John. *The Historical Writings of John Fiske: The Discovery of America*. Vol. 3. 12 vols. New York: Houghton Mifflin, 1902.

Forman, Robert K. C. "Pure Consciousness Events and Mysticism." *Sophia* 25, no. April (1986): 49–58.

Forman, Robert K. S. *Mysticism, Mind, Consciousness*. Albany: State University of New York, 1999. https://amzn.to/2I3Kyl6.

Freeman, A. "The Sense of Being Glared At: What Is It LIke to Be a Heretic?" *Journal of Consciousness Studies* 12, no. 6 (2005): 4–9.

Gandhi, Mohandas Karamchand. *Gandhi: An Autobiography*. Translated by Mahadev Desai. Green Reader Publications, n.d. https://amzn.to/2WnIbjB.

Gasper, Phill. "Jesus the Revolutionary?" *Socialist Worker*, 2011. https://socialistworker.org/2011/12/14/jesus-the-revolutionary.

Giridharadas, Anand. *Winners Take All: The Elite Charade of Changing the World*. New York: Knopf, 2018. https://amzn.to/2FDfF49.

Glass, Andrew. "Reagan Declares 'War on Drugs,' October 14, 1982." Politico, 1992. https://www.politico.com/story/2010/10/reagan-declares-war-on-drugs-october-14-1982-043552.

Griffin, David Ray. "Introduction: The Reenchantment of Science." In *The Reenchantment of Science*, edited by David Ray Griffin, 1–46. New York: State University of New York, 1988.

Grof, Christina, and Stanislav Grof. *The Stormy Search for the Self: A Guide to Personal Growth Through Transformational Crises*. TarcherPerigee, 1992. https://amzn.to/2UtkgP1.

Grof, Stanislav, and Christina Grof. *Spiritual Emergency: When Personal Transformation Becomes a Crises*. New York: Putnam, 1989. https://amzn.to/2KbTh6s.

GrrlScientist. "UN Report: 1 Million Animal And Plant Species At Risk Of Extinction." Forbes. Accessed May 18, 2019. https://www.forbes.com/sites/grrlscientist/2019/05/09/un-report-1-million-animal-and-plant-species-at-risk-of-extinction/.

Hanes, Karl. "Unusual Phenomena Associated With a Transcendent Human Experience: A Case Study." *The Journal of Transpersonal Psychology* 44, no. 1 (2012): 26–47.

Harris, Kylie P., Adam J. Rock, and Gavin I. Clark. "Spiritual Emergency, Psychosis and Personality: A Quantitative Investigation." *Journal of Transpersonal Psychology* 47, no. 2 (July 2015): 263–85.

Harvey, Andrew. *Teachings of the Christian Mystics*. Kindle. Boston: Shambhala Publications, 1998. https://amzn.to/2VrC7CY.

———. *Teachings of the Hindu Mystics*. Kindle. Boston: Shambhala Publications, 2001. https://amzn.to/2WQoduv.

Havens, R. A. "Approaching Cosmic Consciousness via Hypnosis." *Journal of Humanistic Psychology* 22, no. 1 (1982): 105–16.

Hermanns, William. *Einstein and the Poet*. Boston: Branden Books, 1983. https://amzn.to/2EXiooQ.

Hood Jr, Ralph W., Nima Ghorbani, P. J. Watson, Ahad Framarz Ghramaleki, Mark N. Bing, H. Kristl Davison, Ronald J. Morris, and W. Paul Williamson. "Dimensions of the Mysticism Scale: Confirming the Three-Factor Structure in the United States and Iran." *Journal for the Scientific Study of Religion* 40, no. 4 (2001): 691–705.

Hutton, Ronald. *The Druids*. London: Hambledon Continuum, 2007.

Huxley, Aldous. *The Doors of Perception*. Granada Publishing: London, 1984. https://amzn.to/2tXEQYI.

———. *The Perennial Philosophy*. Canada: Random House Canada, 2014. https://amzn.to/2XGmQyM.

Ichazo, Oscar. *The Human Process of Enlightenment and Freedom*. New York: Arica Institute, 1976.

Jacobson, Knut A., ed. "Yoga Powers and Religious Traditions." In *Yoga Powers: Extraordinary Capacities Attained Through Meditation and*

Concentration, 37:1–31. Brill's Indological Library. Boston: Brill, 2012. https://amzn.to/2V8ARsw.

James M. Robinson. *The Nag Hammadi Library: The Definitive New Translation of the Gnostic Scriptures*. Third. San Francisco: Harper, 1988.

James, William. *The Varieties of Religious Experience: A Study of Human Nature*. New York: Penguin, 1982. https://amzn.to/2SQZ7Jv.

Janos, Adam. "What Was It Like to Die of Cyanide Poisoning at Jonestown?" A&E. Accessed June 24, 2019. https://www.aetv.com/real-crime/jonestown-how-did-it-feel-to-die-of-cyanide-poisoning.

Jantzen, Grace M. "Mysticism and Experience." *Religious Studies* 25, no. 3 (1989): 295–315.

Johnson, Harold R. *Firewater: How Alcohol Is Killing My People (and Yours)*. U of R Press, 2016. https://amzn.to/2D142T4.

Julian of Norwich. *Revelations of Divine Love*. Translated by Grace Warrack. Christian Classics Ethereal Library, 1901. https://amzn.to/2I1hnyZ.

Kacela, Xolani. "Being One with the Spirit: Dimensions of a Mystical Experience." *The Journal of Pastoral Care & Counseling* 60, no. 1–2 (Spr 2006): 83–94.

Keen, Sam. "Breaking the Tyranny of the Ego." In *Interviews with Oscar Ichazo*, 3–28. New York: Arica Institute Press, 1982. https://amzn.to/2MOwleU.

Keutzer, Carolyn. "WHATEVER TURNS YOU ON: TRIGGERS TO TRANSCENDENT

EXPERIENCES." *Journal of Humanistic Psychology* 18, no. 3 (1978): 77.

Kohl, Laura Johnston. *Jonestown Survivor*. iUniverse, 2010. https://amzn.to/2WJFtoK.

Lancer, Darlene, JD, and MFT Last updated: 8 Oct 2018~3 min read. "Shame: The Core of Addiction and Codependency." Psych Central, May 17, 2016. https://psychcentral.com/lib/shame-the-core-of-addiction-and-codependency/.

Laszlo, Ervin, Stanislav Grof, and Peter Russell. *The Consciousness Revolution*. Las Vegas: Elf Rock Productions, 1999. https://amzn.to/2TlOCmC.

Layton, Deborah. *Seductive Poison*. New York: Anchor Books, 2010. https://amzn.to/2wxOse4.

Lukoff, David. "The Diagnosis of Mystical Experiences with Psychotic Features." *Journal of Transpersonal Psychology* 17, no. 2 (December 1985): 155.

MacLean, Kenneth. "The Law of Attraction and War." EzineArticles. Accessed June 3, 2019. https://ezinearticles.com/?The-Law-of-Attraction-and-War&id=280965.

Mann, Leslie. "The `cocooning' Trend Draws Reinforcement - Chicago Tribune." Newspaper. Chicago Tribune, 2001. https://www.chicagotribune.com/news/ct-xpm-2001-10-21-0110210261-story.html.

Marshall, Robert. "The Dark Legacy of Carlos Castaneda." Salon, April 12, 2007. https://www.salon.com/2007/04/12/castaneda/.

Maslow, A. H. "Lessons from the Peak-Experiences." *Journal of Humanistic Psychology* 2, no. 1 (January 1, 1962): 9–18. https://doi.org/10.1177/002216786200200102.

———. *Religions, Values, and Peak Experiences*. Columbus: Ohio State University Press, 1964. https://amzn.to/2U2Rhgq.

———. "Some Basic Propositions of a Growth and Self-Actualization Psychoogy." In *Theories of Personality*, edited by G. Lindzey and L. Hall, 307–16. New York: Wiley, 1965.

Maslow, Abraham, and Clark E. Moustakas. "Self-Actualization People: A Study of Psychological Health." In *The Self: Explorations in Personal Growth*, 160–94. Harper Colophon, 1956.

Miller, Russell. *Bare-Faced Messiah: The True Story of L. Ron Hubbard*. London: Silvertail Books, 2015. https://amzn.to/2ESbMI5.

Miller, William R, and Janet C'de Baca. *Quantum Change: When Epiphanies and Sudden Insights Transform Ordinary Lives*. New York: The Guildford Press, 2001. https://amzn.to/2D1gYZo.

Milne, Hugh. *Bhagwan: The God That Failed*. St Martin's Press, 2015. https://amzn.to/2I5MglH.

Miscavige Hill, Jenna. "Beyond Belief: My Secret Life Inside Scientology and My Harrowing Escape EBook: Jenna Miscavige Hill, Lisa Pulitzer: Kindle Store," 2013. https://amzn.to/2W796kl.

Mitha, Karim. "Sufism and Healing." *Journal of Spirituality in Mental Health*, 2018.

Mogar, R. E. "Current Status and Future Trends in Psychedelic (LSD) Research." *Journal of Humanistic Psychology* 2 (1965): 147–66.

Mogar, Robert E., and Charles Savage. "Personality Change Associated with Psychedelic (LSD) Therapy: A Preliminary Report." *Psychotherapy: Theory, Research & Practice* 1, no. 4 (1964): 154–62. https://doi.org/10.1037/h0088594.

Naulty, R. A. "J L Mackie's Disposal of Religious Experience." *Sophia* 31, no. 1 (July 1992): 1–9. https://doi.org/10.1007/BF02772348.

Nededog, Jethro. "How Scientology Costs Members up to Millions of Dollars, According to Leah Remini's Show." Business Insider, 2016. https://www.businessinsider.com/scientology-costs-leah-remini-recap-episode-3-2016-12.

Netherland, Tom. "Doctrine of Forgiveness Vital to Most World Religions." HeraldCourier.com. Accessed August 26, 2019. https://www.heraldcourier.com/lifestyles/doctrine-of-forgiveness-vital-to-most-world-religions/article_b3157727-7aec-5a67-9498-6fc3eac4c188.html.

Newberg, Andrew, Eugene d'Aquile, and Vince Rause. *Why God Won't Go Away: Brain Science and the Biology of Belief*. New York: Ballantine Books, 2001.

Offord, R.M. *Jerry McAuley: An Apostle to the Lost*. New York: Forgotten Books, 2012. https://amzn.to/2UFacCr.

Oregonian, The. "Rajneeshees Establish Security Forces, Large Armory (Part 10 of 20)." oregonlive.com,

July 10, 1985. https://www.oregonlive.com/rajneesh/1985/07/rajneeshees_establish_security.html.

Parish, Bobbi. *Create Your Personal Sacred Text: Develop and Celebrate Your Spiritual Life*. Harmony, 1999. https://amzn.to/2I4zRi7.

Parker, Arthur C. *The Code of Handsome Lake The Seneca Prophet*. Kindle. New York: The University of the State of New York, 1913. https://amzn.to/2H4fr8a.

Persinger, M. A. *Neuropsychological Bases of God Beliefs*. New York: Praeger, 1987.

Powers, Abigail, Negar Fani, Dorthie Cross, Kerry J. Ressler, and Bekh Bradley. "Research Article: Childhood Trauma, PTSD, and Psychosis: Findings from a Highly Traumatized, Minority Sample." *Child Abuse & Neglect* 58 (August 1, 2016): 111–18.

Rahman, Farhat Naz. "Spiritual Healing and Sufi Practices." *Nova Journal of Sufism and Spirituality* 2, no. 1 (2014): 1–9.

Rahtz, Emmylou, Sian Bonnell, Sarah Goldingay, Sara Warber, and Paul Dieppe. "Transformational Changes in Health Status: A Qualitative Exploration of Healing Moments." *EXPLORE* 13, no. 5 (September 1, 2017): 298–305. https://doi.org/10.1016/j.explore.2017.06.005.

Rahula, Walpola Sri. "The First Sermon of the Buddha." Tricycle: The Buddhist Review, 2016. https://tricycle.org/magazine/the-first-sermon-of-the-buddha/.

———. "The Noble Eightfold Path: Meaning and Practice." Tricycle: The Buddhist Review. Accessed April 25, 2019. https://tricycle.org/magazine/noble-eightfold-path/.

Regardie, Israel. *The Tree of Life: An Illustrated Study in Magic*. 2001. Woodbury, Minnesota: Llewellyn, 2001.

Rice, Julian. *Before the Great Spirit: The Many Faces of Sioux Spirituality*. University of New Mexico, 1998. https://amzn.to/2C9fM5E.

Rogers, Carl. *Carl Rogers on Encounter Groups*. Boston: Houghton Mifflin, 1970.

Rountree, Kathryn. "Transforming Deities: Modern Pagan Projects of Revival and Reinvention." *International Journal for the Study of New Religions* 8, no. 2 (July 2017): 213–36.

Ruether, Rosemary Radford. "The Normalization of Goddess Religion." *Feminist Theology* 13, no. 2 (January 2005): 151–57.

Sabbir, Mir. "Burned to Death for Reporting Sexual Harassment." *BBC News*, 2019, sec. Asia. https://www.bbc.com/news/world-asia-47947117.

Sankaracharya. *The Crest-Jewel of Wisdom and Other Writings of Sankaracharya*. Translated by Charles Johnston. Kindle Edition. 1999: Theosophical University Press, 1946. https://www.theosociety.org/pasadena/crest/crest-1.htm.

Sankaracharya, Adi. *The Crest-Jewel of Wisdom*. St. Albert, 2019.

———. *The Crest-Jewel of Wisdom: An LP Annotation*. Alberta: Lightning Path Press, 2019. https://datadump.lightningpath.org/annotations/Crest.Jewel.of.Wisdom-Shankara-Sosteric.pdf.

Schreber, Daniel Paul. *Memoirs of My Nervous Illness*. New York: NYRB Classics, 2000. https://amzn.to/2U8Se6Q.

Shear, Jonathan. "Mysticism and Scientific Naturalism." *Sophia* 43, no. 1 (May 2004): 83–99. https://doi.org/10.1007/BF02782439.

Sosteric, Mike. "A River of Power Runs Through Us." *Culturally Modified*, 2019. https://culturallymodified.org/.

———. "A Sociology of Tarot." *Canadian Journal of Sociology* 39, no. 3 (2014). https://www.academia.edu/25055505/.

———. "Everybody Has a Connection Experience: Prevalence, Confusions, Interference, and Redefinition." *Spirituality Studies* 4, no. 2 (2018). https://www.spirituality-studies.org/dp-volume4-issue2-fall2018/files/assets/common/downloads/files/4-2-sosteric.pdf.

———. "From Zoroaster to Star Wars, Jesus to Marx: The Science and Technology of Mass Human Behaviour," 2018. https://www.academia.edu/34504691.

———. "How Money Is Destroying the World." *The Conversation*, 2018. https://theconversation.com/how-money-is-destroying-the-world-96517.

———. "How the Conservative Right Hijacks Religion." *The Conversation*, 2019.

———. https://theconversation.com/how-the-conservative-right-hijacks-religion-109218.

———. *Lightning Path Workbook One: Basic Concepts*. Vol. 1. Lightning Path Workbook Series. St. Albert, Alberta: Lightning Path Press, 2016. https://press.lightningpath.org/product/the-lightning-path-book-one-authentic-spirituality/.

———. "Mystical Experience and Global Revolution." *Athens Journal of Social Sciences* 5, no. 3 (2018): 235–55.

———. "Power to the People: How the Church Taketh Away." Culturally Modified, 2019. https://culturallymodified.org/power-to-the-people-how-the-church-taketh-away/.

———. "Rethinking the Origins and Purpose of Religion: Jesus, Constantine, and the Containment of Global Revolution," Unpublished. https://www.academia.edu/34970150/.

———. *Rocket Scientists' Guide to Money and the Economy: Accumulation and Debt*. St Albert, Alberta: Lightning Path Press., 2016.

———. "Star Wars Is a Religion That Primes Us for War and Violence." *The Conversation*, 2018. https://theconversation.com/star-wars-is-a-religion-that-primes-us-for-war-and-violence-89443.

———. "The Emotional Abuse of Our Children: Teachers, Schools, and the Sanctioned Violence of Our Modern Institutions." *The Socjournal* March (October 2013).

———. "The Red Pill or the Blue Pill: Endless Consumption or Sustainable Future?" *The Conversation*, 2019. https://theconversation.com/the-red-pill-or-the-blue-pill-endless-consumption-or-sustainable-future-110473.

———. "The Science of Ascension: A Neurologically Grounded Theory of Mystical/Spiritual Experience," 2017.

———. "The Science of Ascension: The Healing Power of Connection," 2016.

———. "The Wild Fox Koan," 2019. https://www.lightningpath.org/readings/the-wild-fox-koan/.

———. "Toxic Socialization." *Socjourn*, 2016. https://www.academia.edu/25275338/Toxic_Socialization.

———. "What Is Socialization." *The Socjourn* (blog), 2019. https://www.sociology.org/what-is-socialization/.

Sosteric, Mike, and Gina Ratkovic. *Lightning Path Workbook Two - Healing*. Vol. 2. Lightning Path Workbook Series. St. Albert, Alberta: Lightning Path Press, 2017. https://press.lightningpath.org/product/the-lightning-path-book-two-healing/.

———. "Seven Essential Needs," 2018. https://www.academia.edu/38114100/The_Seven_Essential_Needs.

St. Teresa of Avila. *Interior Castle*. Kindle. New York: Dover Publications, 2007. https://amzn.to/2GpC7NG.

———. *The Way of Perfection*. New York: Dover Publications, 2012. https://amzn.to/2Id75es.

Stace, Walter Terence. *The Teachings of the Mystics*. New York: Mentor, 1960.

Starhawk. *Spiral Dance, The - 20th Anniversary: A Rebirth of the Ancient Religion of the Goddess: 20th Anniversary Edition: Starhawk: 9780676974676: Gateway - Amazon.Ca*. New York: Harper One, 2011. https://www.amazon.ca/Spiral-Dance-Anniversary-Rebirth-Religion/dp/0062516329/ref=sr_1_1?keywords=the+spiral+dance&qid=1555076627&s=gateway&sr=8-1.

Starr, Bernard. *Jesus Uncensored: Restoring the Authentic Jew*. OmniHouse Publishing, 2013.

Stewart, Gregory B. *Fellow of the Craft; A Treatise on the Second Degree of Freemasonry*. FMI Publishing, 2015.

Suzuki, D.T. *An Introduction to Zen Buddhism*. Grove Press, 1994. https://amzn.to/2Tp6gWG.

"The Placebo Effect: What Is It?" WebMD. Accessed June 26, 2019. https://www.webmd.com/pain-management/what-is-the-placebo-effect.

Thomas, Hobart F. "Self-Actualization through the Group Experience." *Journal of Humanistic Psychology* 4, no. 1 (January 1964): 39.

Tillich, Paul. *Biblical Religion and the Search for Ultimate Reality*. Chicago: University of Chicago Press, 1955. https://amzn.to/2VHLBK6.

Tolstoy, Leo. *The Kingdom of God Is Within You (Classics To Go) EBook: Leo Tolstoy: Amazon.ca: Gateway*.

Translated by Constance Garnett. CreateSpace, 2016. https://amzn.to/2Dg2jtj.

Underhill, Evelyn. *Mysticism: A Study in the Nature and Development of Spiritual Consciousness*. Kindle. New York: Dover Publications, 2002. https://amzn.to/2C91xNY.

Versluis, Arthur. *Magic and Mysticism: An Introduction to Western Esotericism*. Maryland: Rowman and Littlefield, 2007.

———. *The Secret History of Western Sexual Mysticism*. Rochester, Vermont: Destiny Books, 2008.

Watson, J. "Intentionality and Caring-Healing Consciousness: A Practice of Transpersonal Nursing." *Holistic Nursing Practice* 16, no. 4 (2002): 12–19.

Watts, Alan. *This Is It and Other Essays on Zen and Spiritual Experience*. Kindle Edition. Random House, 1973. https://amzn.to/2IYr2rv.

Way, Chapman, and Maclain Way. *Wild Wild Country*. Documentary. Netflix, 2018. https://www.netflix.com/ca/title/80145240.

White, John, ed. *What Is Enlightenment?* St. Paul, MN: Paragon House, 1995. https://amzn.to/3obVany.

White, William L. "Transformational Change: A Historical Review." *Journal of Clinical Psychology* 60, no. 5 (May 2004): 461–70.

Yen, Master Sheng. *Chan and Enlightenment*. Kindle. Taipei: Dharma Drum Publishing, 2014.

Zaehner, R.C. *Hindu and Muslim Mysticism*. New York: Shocken Books, 1969. https://amzn.to/2IK1A7R.

———. *Mysticism Sacred and Profane*. New York: Oxford University Press, 1969. https://amzn.to/2LcdkCl.

Index

Activation. 6, 51, 60, 69, 71, 72, 76, 77, 78, 79, 80, 81, 82, 83, 84, 85, 86, 89, 90, 91, 92, 95, 96, 97, 98, 99, 100, 101, 102, 110, 112, 114, 116, 132, 133, 150, 164, 166, 170, 176

Alignment Manual 110

Ascension Manual 6, 18, 83, 84, 85, 110, 111, 116, 117, 118, 119, 120, 121, 122, 134, 137, 138, 158, 166, 168, 169, 172, 173

Bhagwan Shree Rajneesh 18, 113, 173

Bodily ego 8, 66, 102, 103, 104, 111, 117, 162

Caring Moments 56

Connection Manual 78, 110

Connection outcomes. 6, 28, 46, 48, 49, 50, 51, 53, 100, 101, 112, 113, 116, 120, 132, 135, 144, 182, 198

Connection practice 57, 103, 117, 118, 160, 178, 179

Consciousness effect 58, 59

Cosmic consciousness 28, 48, 64, 65, 138, 177

Council of Hippo 125

Death tests 35, 36, 38, 39

Direct labour 13

Ego explosion 110

Epiphanies 49, 63, 101

Existential terrors 110

External resistance 6, 81, 85, 86, 87, 90, 91, 97

Fabric of Consciousness 8, 21, 44, 47, 102, 103

Flooding 110

Healing.6, 10, 48, 51, 53, 54, 55, 56, 57, 59, 60, 62, 78, 88, 89, 100, 101, 104, 105, 112, 116, 118, 143, 145, 154, 176, 198

Healing experiences 48, 51, 56

Healing Moments 56

Humanistic psychology 88, 89

Illuminations 63

Indirect labour 13, 14

Internal Resistance 91

Less Than Messages 96

Life tests 36, 37, 38, 39

Mantle of Spiritual Authority 17, 136

Mental purification 98, 100

Nadir experience 65, 66, 68, 69, 97

Noble Eightfold Path 99

Nomenclature confusion 6, 27, 29, 34, 51, 113

Oppression 95

Peak experiences 47, 51, 64, 65, 66, 88

Physical unit 7, 8, 156, 157, 159, 160

Pure Conscious Events 64

Quantum Change 78

Revelations 49, 64, 153

Right action 52, 112

Right environment 52, 112, 162

Right thought 52, 99, 112

Satori Experiences 64

Toxic socialization 66, 92, 95, 104, 157, 158, 159

Transcendence 88

Transformation Experiences 56

Transformational change	78
Union experience	103
Unity experiences	47
Wrong Action	52
Wrong Environment	52
Wrong thought	52, 104
Zenith experience	63

www.ingramcontent.com/pod-product-compliance
Lightning Source LLC
LaVergne TN
LVHW051550070426
835507LV00021B/2506